DURABLE JOY

Mysteriously Hidden in Plain Sight

DURABLE JOY

Mysteriously Hidden in Plain Sight

JOHN SEARS

A Division of WINEPRESS PUBLISHING

ISBN 1-57921-540-8
Library of Congress Catalog Card Number: 2002116004

Table of Contents

The Search for Durable Joy 7

It Looks Backwards 11

Born Again 19

Belonging 25

Faith 37

Baptisms 47

Fruit of the Holy Spirit 61

Gifts of the Holy Spirit 73

The Whole Armor of God 87

B-Team 103

Tongues of Men and Angels 117

Essentials of Prayer 133

Brokenness 145

Boldness 153

Blessings 165

Backsliding 175

Joy in Worship 183

Bema Rewards 197

Joy Without End, Amen 207

Chapter 1

The Search for Durable Joy

Hidden in Plain Sight

> Verily, verily, I say unto you . . . your sorrow shall be turned into joy.
> *John 16:20*

Opening Prayer: Lord, I can't figure out why the world looks so crazy and cruel, and I'm not sure how you can give me joy in the midst of this turmoil. Please open my eyes and my mind to understand Your plan and grasp what's missing in my life.

The secret of joy isn't buried somewhere deep underground. It's hidden in plain sight, where any child can find it.

It's been sitting there for nearly 2,000 years, available to anybody willing to accept it. Some receive it, but most people walk right by, unwilling to believe that joy can be so simple.

True joy is strangely durable, able to withstand the hardships of real life. Unlike happiness, which depends on what *happens* to me, joy comes from a completely reliable source: God Himself. This truth is plainly stated in Psalm 16:

11 Thou wilt show me the path of life: in thy presence is fulness of joy; at thy right hand there are pleasures for evermore.

Despite the evidence that joy comes from God, joy was a mystery to me for nearly 30 years. I had passionately searched for happiness in sports, in relationships, in religion, in music and countless other places. There were moments of pleasure, but nothing that brought lasting joy.

Finally I decided to watch people who had joy and see how *they* got it. Their trail led me to Jesus and then disappeared. Did Jesus have something to do with their joy?

Getting to joy

The joyful people told me how to solve the mystery, but I didn't get it right away. I was being too logical and too religious.

Eventually it dawned on me: God has nothing to say to religious people. His plan can only be understood by people humble enough to be taught and transformed by the Holy Spirit.

The joyful people told me that I could not obtain joy directly. They told me that joy was a character trait, like patience and gentleness. They said that joy would be produced in my heart by the working of the Holy Spirit. To prove this, they quoted from the fifth chapter of Paul's letter to the Galatians:

22 But the fruit of the Spirit is love, joy, peace, longsuffering, gentleness, goodness, faith, 23 Meekness, temperance: against such there is no law.

By this time, my logical mind was getting impatient. If joy could only be produced by the Holy Spirit working in my heart, then what was He waiting for? Why didn't I already have 30 years worth of mature fruit as a result of His working?

The joyful people patiently explained that the Holy Spirit doesn't produce this fruit in every human being. He only cultivates hearts that have been consciously dedicated to the Lordship of Jesus Christ.

At this point, I began to get irritated at the joyful people. Were they implying that I was *not* a Christian? How could they say that? I had spent many years attending various Christian churches, and had put a lot of conscious effort into trying to be a good person. Didn't that make me a Christian?

The joyful people said I needed to give my heart to Jesus and be "born again." That was really offensive to my logical mind. Maybe some seven-year-old kid could accept that explanation, but not a 30-year-old college graduate. It was too simple. It was hidden in plain sight.

Only one fact kept me coming back: these people had the evidence of God's handiwork in their character. They had joy and I did not. These people knew the Bible well, and I did not.

So I asked for more detail about God's plan to give us joy. My logical mind needed more structure.

God's Mysterious Plan

The joyful people said that the key was to study Jesus and His teachings. They said that Jesus hid the truth in plain sight by teaching in parables. Most people who heard Him went home mystified. Even his disciples were confused at first, as we read in the fourth chapter of Mark's Gospel:

> [10] And when He was alone, they who were about Him, with the Twelve, asked Him concerning the parable. [11] And He said to them, "To you it is given to know the mystery of the kingdom of God. But to those outside, all these things are given in parables [12] so that seeing they may see, and not perceive; and hearing they may hear, and not understand; lest at any time they should be converted, and their sins should be forgiven them."

Eventually the disciples came to understand, but it took them awhile to grasp Jesus' plan for their lives.

The disciples struggled for the same reason that I struggled, because God's plan is based on *His* logic, not human logic. And His logic seems backwards until we get used to it.

For nearly 2,000 years, the Gospel message has puzzled people. The Apostle Paul predicted this in his first letter to the church at Corinth:

> [1:18] For the preaching of the cross is foolishness to them that are perishing; but unto us which are saved it is the power of God.

The Gospel message looks foolish because God designed it to be a mystery. In the second chapter of 1 Corinthians we read:

[7] But we speak *the* **wisdom of God in a mystery**, which God has hidden, predetermining it before the world for our glory; [8] which none of the rulers of this world knew (for if they had known, they would not have crucified the Lord of glory). [9] But as it is written, "Eye has not seen, nor ear heard," nor has it entered into the heart of man, "the things which God has prepared for those who love Him." [10] But God has revealed *them* to us by His Spirit; for the Spirit searches all things, yea, the deep things of God. (*MKJV*)

The Holy Spirit wants to teach us and transform our lives. Until we have been transformed and taught in the ways of the Lord, the Gospel message looks very foolish to us. The very next verses of the same chapter say:

[12] But we have not received the spirit of the world, but the Spirit from God, so that we might know the things that are freely given to us by God. [13] These things we also speak, not in words which man's wisdom teaches, but which the Holy Spirit teaches, comparing spiritual things with spiritual. [14] But the natural man does not receive the things of the Spirit of God, for they are foolishness to him; neither can he know them, because they are spiritually discerned. (*MKJV*)

For years, I had thought that "born-again" Christianity looked pretty foolish. These verses, however, suggested that I had misunderstood something along the way. So I decided to buy a Bible and research whether the Scriptures supported the plan described by the joyful people.

If you have thought that Christianity seems foolish, you've come to the right place. The remaining chapters of this book will help you understand God's peculiar plan as explained in the Bible.

If you're already a "born-again" believer but haven't experienced enough joy lately, keep reading. This book will help you be sure you aren't skipping any steps.

Closing Prayer: Heavenly Father, I don't pretend to understand Your wisdom or Your perfect plan. Help me to distinguish between the plan described in Your Scriptures and the religious nonsense proposed by everybody else. Guide me and protect me and lead me in Your truth, I pray. Amen.

Chapter 2

It Looks Backwards

Am I Upright or Upside Down?

For my thoughts *are* not your thoughts, neither *are* your ways my ways, saith the LORD. *Isaiah 55:8*

Opening Prayer: Heavenly Father, Your ways seem pretty mysterious, but I'm willing to learn more. Help me understand Your plan and what I should do about it, I pray. Amen.

The joyful people assured me that God's plan calls for us to walk uprightly and be like Him. They said His way can be taught to any child (and some adults), as King David wrote in Psalm 25:

⁸ Good and upright *is* the LORD: therefore will He teach sinners in the way. ⁹ The meek will He guide in judgment: and the meek will He teach his way.

God Himself has promised to teach us His ways. So He sent His Son, Jesus, to be our Teacher and our Lord. Jesus told people about God's plan, but He spoke in parables. Some people recognized that Jesus spoke with power and authority and followed Him. Others were too invested in their religion to recognize Him as their Messiah.

Jesus did not come to establish a religion. He wants a relationship with you, as we see in the 11th chapter of Matthew's gospel:

> 28 Come unto me, all ye that labour and are heavy laden, and I will give you rest.

Jesus doesn't care whether you're rich or poor, religious or not. He calls you to give up your self-centered or denomination-centered belief system and follow Him:

> 29 Take my yoke upon you, and learn of me; for I am meek and lowly in heart: and ye shall find rest unto your souls; 30 for my yoke is easy, and my burden is light.

Jesus promised supernatural joy and rest to those who follow Him. But His program looked really backwards to my logical mind. Especially challenging was this quote from the sixteenth chapter of John's gospel:

> 33 These things I have spoken unto you, that in me ye might have peace. In the world ye shall have tribulation: but be of good cheer; I have overcome the world.

Jesus made an amazing two-part prediction in the verse above. He predicted that we will have great difficulties in life, but that He can give us inner peace despite these difficulties.

Obviously the first part is true: life is really hard. Some days it's unbelievably painful. But Jesus claimed He could give us genuine peace, not just pain-management skills.

So?

I could not leave such outrageous claims unchallenged, and neither can you. You must test His crazy promise for yourself, in your own life. You must investigate what the Bible says about Jesus' plan for your life and make an informed decision.

Even though God's way is simple, the "how-to" aspects seem very peculiar at first glance. Jesus gave us a difficult lesson in the Beatitudes, explaining what types of people receive joy and blessings. In the gospel of Matthew, chapter 5, we read:

³ Blessed *are* the poor in spirit, for theirs is the kingdom of Heaven. ⁴ Blessed *are* those who mourn, for they shall be comforted. ¹¹ Blessed are you when they revile and persecute you, and say all kinds of evil against you falsely for My sake. ¹² Rejoice and be exceedingly glad, for great is your reward in Heaven, for so they persecuted the prophets who were before you. (NKJV)

Human logic and emotion tell you to shrink away from all of these "blessed" conditions. Nobody *wants* to be poor or to mourn. Nobody *wants* to be reviled and persecuted. But Jesus tells us that those who suffer for His sake will receive blessings.

It gets worse. Not only are the greatest blessings received from the worst circumstances, but most people will think you're crazy. Most people are trying desperately to find an easy road to happiness—and aren't finding it. Their only consolation is that everybody else they know is doing the same stuff.

Good Company

Jesus removed even that slim consolation in Matthew chapter 7:

¹³ Go in through the narrow gate, for wide is the gate and broad is the way that leads to destruction, and many there are who go in through it. ¹⁴ Because narrow is the gate and constricted is the way which leads to life, and there are few who find it. (MKJV)

Does this statement shock you? It should.

Jesus declares that most people will not get into Heaven. Most of the people you know are choosing the easy road to destruction. They will not approve if you choose to break ranks with them.

Harsh as it sounds, your former (worldly) support system will *not* support you through the narrow gate. They liked you better when you were clueless and comfortable on the broad road to Hell. A few friends may follow your example to follow Jesus, but don't be surprised at the widening gap between you and the others.

Jesus declares that the road to Hell is wide, comfortable and well-traveled. Many of your friends and family are blindly following the enemy down that road. The enemy has disguised that road by making it appear like a thousand different spiritual paths, many of them pretending to be Christian.

Jesus declares that the road to Heaven is narrow, and that you can only make it by following Him. There is no third road. Just two. The narrow one goes to Heaven, and the other goes to Hell. You must pick one. God will honor your choice, even if your friends do not.

Success

The third difficult lesson concerned the road to "success." Jesus made it clear that joy does not depend on our political or financial accomplishments, as we read in Matthew 18:

> [1] At that time the disciples came to Jesus, saying, "Who then is greatest in the kingdom of Heaven?" [2] Then Jesus called a little child to Him, set him in the midst of them, [3] and said, "Assuredly, I say to you, unless you are converted and become as little children, you will by no means enter the kingdom of Heaven. [4] Therefore whoever humbles himself as this little child is the greatest in the kingdom of Heaven." (*NKJV*)

This lesson caused me some personal discomfort because of my previous involvement with the "positive attitude" and religious science movements. For years, I had believed that my own words had creative power and that I was evolving toward becoming a higher life form in my next incarnation. Why should I be humble if I was in the process of becoming a god? I thought I was tapping into the "Christ principle" within myself, and I thought Jesus would approve.

Instead, Jesus spoke of a process whereby grown persons are converted (the Greek word is *strepho* meaning "turned around") and changed. As a healthy child has a healthy respect of adults, a healthy Christian walks in humility in view of the awesome power and perfection of almighty God. God is so high above us that we can't even worry if people around us are "higher" or "lower" than us.

In the same vein, I had previously believed that material riches were proof of God's approval. This notion was dispelled in Matthew 19:

> [23] Then Jesus said to His disciples, "Assuredly, I say to you that it is hard for a rich man to enter the kingdom of Heaven. [24] "And again I say to you, it is easier for a camel to go through the eye of a needle than for a rich man to enter the kingdom of God." [25] When His disciples heard it, they were greatly astonished, saying, "Who then can

be saved?" [26] But Jesus looked at them and said to them, "With men this is impossible, but with God all things are possible." *(NKJV)*

The narrow gate is just wide enough for one person at a time. Any of us can pass through it, one person at a time. The narrow gate is *not* wide enough to accommodate people carrying baggage. If you value any person or thing higher than Jesus, then that person or thing has become an idol. Leave him/her/it in God's hands and follow Jesus through the gate.

The principle is easy to understand, but hard to accept. Our human nature wants rewards *now*. God's plan is to reward us *later*. Our human nature wants to achieve and be recognized as Number One in our chosen field. God's plan is to elevate the humble and to humble those who have been prominent and successful in this life.

One or the Other

What's even crazier is that Jesus views salvation as an all-or-nothing proposition. Either we receive salvation as a free gift or we choose eternity in Hell. There is nothing in between—except this life. According to the Bible, there is no Limbo or Purgatory or Hell-Lite.

Jesus illustrated the all-or-nothing nature of salvation with the parable of the landowner hiring laborers for his vineyard. At the beginning of the day, he contracted to pay each a day's wage (a denarius). Later in the day, he found other job seekers and hired them—including one group of workers recruited just an hour before quitting time. These latter workers received a denarius, so the initial hires complained about not receiving more, as we see in Matthew 20:

> [12] 'These last men have worked only one hour, and you made them equal to us who have borne the burden and the heat of the day.' [13] "But he answered one of them and said, 'Friend, I am doing you no wrong. Did you not agree with me for a denarius? [14] Take what is yours and go your way. I wish to give to this last man the same as to you. [15] Is it not lawful for me to do what I wish with my own things? Or is your eye evil because I am good?' [16] "So the last will be first, and the first last. For many are called, but few chosen." *(NKJV)*

Remember that we're talking about salvation here. God *does* promise to give us certain rewards based upon our faith in times of trial, but salvation is "yes" or "no," all or nothing.

Don't imagine that famous religious leaders will necessarily get greater rewards than you—or that they'll even *be* in Heaven. Some of them are merely famous and religious, caught up in the external trappings of prestige and power. To be sure that you and I don't miss the point, Jesus returns to this subject in Matthew 23:

> ¹¹ But he who is greatest among you shall be your servant. ¹² And whoever exalts himself will be humbled, and he who humbles himself will be exalted. *(NKJV)*

Actually, this verse should speak comfort to our hearts. We have all suffered at the hands of bullies and proud enemies. Take heart: their talk irritates God, too.

So Where Do I Start?

Jesus made it clear that the Christian walk requires major changes in a person's life. His first words of warning—in fact His first recorded words of public ministry—are found in Matthew 4:

> ¹⁷ From that time Jesus began to preach, and to say, "**Repent**, for the kingdom of Heaven is at hand." ¹⁸ And Jesus, walking by the sea of Galilee, saw two brethren, Simon called Peter, and Andrew his brother, casting a net into the sea: for they were fishers. ¹⁹ And He said unto them, "**Follow Me**, and I will make you fishers of men." *(NKJV)*

From the very beginning, Jesus made it clear that we all need to repent as a first step. Repent is a simple word. It translates the Greek word *metanoeo* meaning to think differently enough to begin acting differently.

But repenting is more than stopping the harmful stuff, or just turning away from our former belief systems. Jesus immediately added the command, "Follow Me!" Repentance causes us to turn *from* one thing and turn *toward* another.

Repentance was a difficult assignment for me. I felt like I had previously done a pretty good job of following Jesus. I had attended church, put money in the offering basket, cut down on my bad language, and had been a law-abiding citizen. I don't feel like a "bad" person.

But I had not received that supernatural implant of new life that Jesus called being "born again." I had not submitted my heart to the life-changing power of the Holy Spirit. My heart had not been transformed and conformed to His image. I did not have the durable joy of the joyful people.

Without that implant of new life, I was not a "bad" person; I was a "dead" person.

I wanted that new life, but had trouble believing the joyful people at first. I had wasted several years following religious phonies. How could I be sure the narrow path was the right path?

Fortunately, my doubts led me to do the right thing. I decided to read the Scriptures for myself and see if the joyful people were right. It took several months of study, because I was too proud to accept their explanation. It was too simple. It was hidden in plain sight.

The next three chapters explain what I discovered about salvation. If you fully grasp the next few chapters, you can be sure of your salvation and receive the durable joy that God promises you.

Let me encourage you to keep reading.

Closing prayer: Father, I can't understand the Gospel message with my human understanding, and I know I can't live up to the Beatitudes. But I'm willing to change. Please help me understand Your plan of salvation and Your plan to transform my heart, I pray in Jesus' name. Amen.

Chapter 3

Born Again

Your New Life Starts *Here*

"I will give you a new heart and put a new spirit within you." *Ezekiel 36:26*

Opening prayer: Father, despite my best efforts, my life comes short of even my own standards. Please open my eyes to see what You will do to and through me if I permit You.

The Bible says that God has a plan for our lives, but what we've seen of it seems pretty backwards. And what about all the violence in this world? Living in a big city, I've sometimes felt trapped behind enemy lines.

I was surprised to learn what Scripture says about our world. It explains that today's thugs and terrorists are being manipulated by an invisible enemy, sometimes called the devil.

You cannot make peace with this enemy, who hates you without a cause. Therefore you must learn to fight back and protect yourself. Unfortunately, physical strength, physical weapons, diplomacy and human intellect are powerless to cope with our invisible, relentless enemy.

Military weapons won't stop our enemy. If you bomb all his follow-ers into ashes, the enemy will simply recruit a fresh batch of lunatics. Likewise all man-made religions are powerless to help you, since they are based on philosophy rather than power.

Since our enemy is spiritual and the real battle is in the realm of the spirit, we need spiritual help in order to survive.

The Gospel (literally "Good News") message is that God wants to give us an implant of His Holy Spirit, a new nature that can be nurtured and developed.

This new nature *can* see into the realm of the spirit world, and *does* have power against the invisible enemy. This new nature *can* give us joy despite our circumstances.

More importantly, this new nature is our passport to Heaven. With-out this new nature, we will lose the spiritual battle here on earth *and* spend eternity on the losing side, surrounded by other losers.

Born From Above

This is a difficult concept. It is completely backwards from every-thing I learned in college. In short, the Bible says we cannot save our-selves by our own efforts. We need a complete "life transplant" to survive.

Our Lord Himself expressed this principle in John 3 verses 3 through 6:

> [3] Jesus answered and said to him, "Most assuredly, I say to you, unless one is born again, he cannot see the kingdom of God." [4] Nicodemus said to Him, "How can a man be born when he is old? Can he enter a second time into his mother's womb and be born?" [5] Jesus answered, "Most assuredly, I say to you, unless one is born of water and the Spirit, he cannot enter the kingdom of God. [6] That which is born of the flesh is flesh, and that which is born of the Spirit is spirit." (*NKJV*)

This is an important principle. Ordinary flesh life can be very nice at times, but it won't get anybody into Heaven. Furthermore, ordinary flesh life will constantly betray us in the midst of the spiritual battle that rages around us today.

Jesus promised a new nature. If we choose to receive and nurture it, will inevitably transform our lives. God's own Spirit will give us a new heart, a renewed mind, and the power to make a difference in the lives of other people. It sounds backwards, but it's effective.

What do you mean "backwards?"

For starters, there are four elements that make the Gospel seem backwards from worldly philosophy:

- **It works indirectly.** Very little in God's kingdom is achieved by the head-on, direct approach. Jesus says the first shall be last and the last shall be first. He who would be greatest of all must first be servant of all. He who exalts himself will be humbled; he who humbles himself will be exalted. Most importantly, we gain salvation when we stop trying to earn it by our own merits and begin trusting in the completed work of Jesus.

- **It works by displacement.** Being "born again" means receiving an implant of supernatural life that we didn't have before—life which must be fed and nurtured. Yet our old sinful nature wages war against our new nature, and continually strives to divert our attention. Spiritual growth depends on consciously choosing to feed the new nature and starve the old. No man can serve two masters or two natures. One nature *will* outgrow and displace the other, as light displaces darkness.

- **It works by power.** God's life-changing power can transform us from the inside out, if we feed our new nature and submit to the leading of the Holy Spirit. In our own strength, all we can do is act religious and go to Hell with all the other religious folks.

- **Upright living *looks* different.** The transforming power of God enables us to walk uprightly, in the light of God's love, on the straight and narrow path. All the rest of the world prefers darkness and "diversity"—another term for the wide, well-traveled paths that lead to destruction. If we walk uprightly, we will look upside down and backwards to our neighbors who don't yet know which way is up.

This way *up*

Let's look for guidance in Paul's letter to the Romans, Chapter 1, verses 16–17:

> [16] For I am not ashamed of the gospel of Christ: for it is the power of God unto salvation to every one that believeth; to the Jew first, and

also to the Greek. [17] For therein is the righteousness of God revealed from faith to faith: as it is written, The just shall live by faith.

Paul hits several key points in quick succession here:

- **He is not ashamed to stand up and proclaim the gospel** (literally "the good news") of Christ (literally "the anointed one"— the Messiah). He's ready to preach even in Rome, where the snobbish power elite will ridicule him and the government will eventually kill him.

- **This gospel involves God's miracle-working power.** The gospel is not a clever collection of words and ideas. There is life-changing power available to do a work in somebody.

- **The work is salvation.** The gospel promises a life-changing implant of the Holy Spirit, being born again, being saved *from* the eternal consequences of sin, being saved *to* the eternal kingdom of God.

- **This power and this work are available freely to *everyone* who believes.** Anyone that exercises faith in the completed work of Jesus, the Messiah of Israel, will receive the life-giving power.

How is *that* faith different from what I'm doing now?

In our culture, "faith" is defined as any type of intellectual belief system. The English language permits "faith" to be a mental exercise, sterile and lifeless as a museum exhibit.

The languages of the Bible, both Hebrew and Greek, do not permit such slothfulness. Both languages use these words as action verbs, not just nouns.

All of my previous religions required a continuous stream of good works in order to merit eternal rewards. They assured me that good people all go to Heaven.

By contrast, the Bible tells us that we can't possibly be good enough to merit Heaven. In the Old Testament, God commanded daily, weekly and annual animal sacrifices to atone for (cover up) our sin. In the New Testament, Jesus gave Himself once and for all as the atoning sacrifice.

Our sins pose a real dilemma for us. It feels *backwards* to say "no" to our favorite sin, in hopes of pleasing a God we can't directly see. But sin is sin. Every type of sin is a deviation from God's standards. The Greek word for sin is *hamartia,* meaning to come short or to miss the mark, like archers failing to hit the target. Our sins, then, are just our short-comings.

Each of us has a treasured set of shortcomings. Some folks struggle with lying. Some struggle with stealing. Some struggle with drinking or drugs. Some struggle with lust. Some struggle with anger and violence. Some have eating disorders. If you tell me you don't struggle with any-thing, then your problem is lying.

All sin is harmful to the sinner and to the community. Some sin (murder, adultery, rape, homosexuality, idolatry) is so damaging to the moral fabric of the community that God commanded the nation of Is-rael to stone the offenders.

Now remember that the kingdom of God works by displacement. Instead of criticizing sin, let us build up our new nature, which can displace the weak, sinful nature we're born with.

Whether *your* particular weakness is violence, substance abuse or lust, it's a waste of time to say, "God *made* me this way." God's original design (with Adam and Eve) was perfection in paradise. Sin changed all that, and the consequences of sin have wreaked havoc on humanity's gene pool.

God's solution for sin is a life-changing heart transplant (being born again), accompanied by life-changing power. If you were born warped (hint: we *all* were), then you need to be born again. All of us can freely partake of that life-changing experience *if we choose to.*

The problem is not that God's plan is too difficult to understand or too hard to accomplish. The problem is that we're willing to try almost anything to avoid submitting to God and His plan.

So how do we take advantage of God's plan? The next chapter, "Be-longing" explains how.

Closing Prayer: Father, I *think* I understand Your plan this far, but it sure sounds different from what I thought it was. Please help me, by Your Holy Spirit, to understand Your plan for my life and how it dif-fers from man-made religious traditions. Amen.

Durable Joy

Chapter 4

Belonging

God's grace ensures your place

[8] For by grace are ye saved through faith; and that not of yourselves: it is the gift of God: [9] Not of works, lest any man should boast. *Ephesians 2:8–9*

Opening Prayer: Heavenly Father, I know that You are smarter and wiser than me, because You created this world and all living creatures. I don't understand why You gave me the gift of life, and I don't understand Your plan for my eternal future. Please open my heart and mind to grasp Your love for me and what I should do next because of Your love. Amen.

The joyful people assured me that my eternal future depended on something called "grace." They said that if I got it right, my joy could begin immediately and last forever.

At first, it was difficult to understand the differences between grace and some other concepts such as justice, mercy, fairness, right or wrong. Let's spend a few minutes explaining what I learned about the other words first and come back to the concept of grace.

Justice

Justice is receiving exactly what you deserve, no more and no less. Justice implies a system of laws, supported by an authorized law-enforcement system. Perfect justice means that every lawbreaker is swiftly caught and punished. It also implies that innocent people are never wrongfully punished. The word first appears in Genesis 18, as God is describing Abraham:

> ¹⁹ For I know him, that he will command his children and his household after him, and they shall keep the way of the LORD, **to do justice and judgment**; that the LORD may bring upon Abraham that which he hath spoken of him.

God knew that Abraham had great personal integrity, and that he would not only *keep* God's law but also *teach* it to his family and *enforce* it in his household and his community.

Mercy

Mercy is forgiveness or leniency toward a person or group that is guilty of breaking a law (sinning). The lawbreakers deserve a specific punishment, but receive mercy in the form of reduced punishment or a complete pardon. The word merciful first appears in Genesis 19:

> ¹⁵ And when the morning arose, then the angels hastened Lot, saying, Arise, take thy wife, and thy two daughters, which are here; lest thou be consumed in the iniquity of the city. ¹⁶ And while he lingered, the men laid hold upon his hand, and upon the hand of his wife, and upon the hand of his two daughters; **the LORD being merciful unto him**; and they brought him forth, and set him without the city.

The city of Sodom was guilty of flagrant sin, and Lot was not completely innocent of Sodom's guilt. Lot had become comfortable as a man of wealth and power in Sodom. Lot *preferred* God's way of doing things, but had become soft and carnal.

The angels came to rescue Lot as a *favor* to Abraham. However, the Bible says that Lot lingered—unwilling to distance himself from his comfortable life in Sin City. The angels could have marched out in disgust and left them all behind. Nevertheless, the angels *showed God's mercy* to Lot by dragging him and his family away from Sodom.

Fairness

Fairness is having every person treated equally under the law, regardless of the differences in age, character, race, economic status, attitude, accomplishments, prior behavior or personal charm. The noisy, complaining brat receives exactly the same allowance as the hardworking, quiet, compliant child. The frivolous lawsuits of a convicted felon are given the same weight as those of honest citizens.

Communism is the theoretical epitome of fairness; everybody gets the same income regardless of what he or she actually contributes to the community. Fairness allows no favorites and rewards no excellence.

Fairness is a concept dear to modern society, but is not a biblical concept. The Bible speaks of *justice* (described above), but the word "fair" normally refers to physical appearance in the King James Version.

Right and Wrong

Right and wrong are determined by law. Right is compliance with the law. Wrong is breaking the law, knowingly or unknowingly.

Notice that all these concepts imply the existence of a legal system. Without law, there is no framework for justice, mercy, fairness, right or wrong. All these concepts depend on the legal system for their contextual meaning. In an Islamic country, "justice" means imprisonment or execution for people who are proven "guilty" of believing in Jesus or making friends with Jewish people.

The Bible explains God's concept of right and wrong. The Bible gives us a thorough picture of God's Law, with examples of good and bad performance. Best of all, the Bible tells us about Jesus, who complied with every aspect of the Law and was absolutely innocent before God. Jesus qualified for Heaven on His own merits.

Unfortunately, you and I are not capable of meeting every requirement of the Law, from birth to death. We have already sinned, and are sure to fail in the future.

Our performance will always come short of God's standard, which is perfection. Perfect justice, then, requires eternal punishment for our shortcomings, because the Law says, "The soul that sinneth shall die." (Ezekiel 18:20) You and I qualify for Hell on our own merits.

Backwards as it sounds, God gave us a Big Loophole: an escape clause from the sentence of death that Justice demands. The Big Loophole enables us to get the Heaven that Jesus deserved, because Jesus paid the punishment that *we* deserved. That is not fair. That is an example of God's grace.

Now we can define grace

Grace—sometimes called "unmerited favor"—means receiving a benefit or reward that we did not earn or deserve to receive. It is a gift.

The first appearance of grace in the Scripture is in Genesis 6, verses 6–8:

> [6] And it repented the LORD that He had made man on the earth, and it grieved Him at His heart. [7] And the LORD said, I will destroy man whom I have created from the face of the earth; both man, and beast, and the creeping thing, and the fowls of the air; for it repenteth me that I have made them. [8] But Noah **found grace** in the eyes of the LORD.

Notice that God, the great Lawgiver, was grieved because of the sins of men. Men were violating whatever Law was available to the human race before the Flood. Noah wasn't perfect, but he had a healthy relationship with God. Noah actively sought to please God, and found grace in God's eyes.

Grace means receiving a benefit because the recipient pleases (finds favor with) God. The term also applies to finding favor in the eyes of an earthly ruler, as we see in Genesis 39:

> [1] And Joseph was brought down to Egypt; and Potiphar, an officer of Pharaoh, captain of the guard, an Egyptian, bought him of the hands of the Ishmaelites, which had brought him down thither. [2] And the LORD was with Joseph, and he was a prosperous man; and he was in the house of his master the Egyptian. [3] And his master saw that the LORD *was* with him, and that the LORD made all that he did to prosper in his hand. [4] And **Joseph found grace in his sight**, and he served him: and he made him overseer over his house, and all *that* he had he put into his hand. [5] And it came to pass from the time *that* he had made him overseer in his house, and over all that he had, that the LORD blessed the Egyptian's house for Joseph's sake; and the blessing of the LORD was upon all that he had in the house, and in the field.

In this example, Joseph had a *right* to become bitter and turn against God. He had not been treated *fairly* by his brothers. But he continued to trust and worship the God of Abraham, Isaac and Jacob. Joseph *found grace* in the eyes of God. In turn, Joseph *found grace* in the eyes of his Egyptian master, Potiphar.

The term also applies to finding favor in the eyes of a person of nearly equal stature, as in Genesis 32:

> ³ And Jacob sent messengers before him to Esau his brother unto the land of Seir, the country of Edom. ⁴ And he commanded them, saying, Thus shall ye speak unto my lord Esau; Thy servant Jacob saith thus, I have sojourned with Laban, and stayed there until now: ⁵ And I have oxen, and asses, flocks, and menservants, and womenservants: and I have sent to tell my lord, **that I may find grace in thy sight.**

Jacob and Esau were approximately equal in terms of stature in their communities. But Esau held the upper hand in terms of power. Esau controlled the land of his father, Isaac, and was able to muster 400 men to meet Jacob.

Some important concepts have already emerged:

- Grace always flows from the greater to the lesser.
- Grace can be sought from earthly rulers as well as from God.
- In each case, the person in power can *expect* a certain amount of obedience and deference because of their relationship. God can *demand* perfect obedience to His will. Potiphar could *demand* obedience from Joseph. Esau's army of 400 men could have *forced* Jacob to settle in another region far away, or even destroyed the entire household.
- In each case, the person seeking grace does more than the minimum expected.

We see an amazing interchange between God and Moses in Exodus 33:

> ¹² Then Moses said to the Lord, "See, You say to me, 'Bring up this people.' But You have not let me know whom You will send with me. Yet You have said, 'I know you by name, and **you have also found grace** in My sight.'" ¹³ "Now therefore, I pray, **if I have found grace** in Your sight, show me now Your way, that I may know You and that I may **find grace** in Your sight. And consider that this nation is Your people." ¹⁴ And He said, "My Presence will go with you, and I will give

you rest." [15] Then he said to Him, "If Your Presence does not go with us, do not bring us up from here. [16] "For how then will it be known that Your people and I have **found grace** in Your sight, except You go with us? So we shall be separate, Your people and I, from all the people who are upon the face of the earth." [17] So the Lord said to Moses, "I will also do this thing that you have spoken; for **you have found grace** in My sight, and I know you by name." (*NKJV*)

This conversation reinforces several of the earlier points: that grace flows from greater to lesser, that the greater can *expect* deference from the lesser, and that the person seeking grace does *more* than the minimum required. We can learn more from this conversation:

- Grace flows out of a relationship. Moses had spent years cultivating his relationship with God.

- Because of the relationship, Moses knew he could ask for certain *favors* from God.

- Moses was *interceding* to obtain two outcomes that were obviously near to God's heart. Moses was first asking God to show His ways to Moses, so Moses could provide inspired leadership to Israel. Second, Moses was asking God to "go with" Israel: to be available to the Israelites on a personal level, and to empower their army on a national level.

- Moses was not trying to change God's mind. He was *interceding* to obtain the best possible outcome, out of the range of outcomes that God would permit.

If you grasp this principle of intercession, it will change your life.

"I thought that only super heroes like Moses can talk to God like this."

That's what I thought. But the Bible says that talking to God *makes* ordinary people into super heroes.

This Scripture passage hints that God has a range of possible outcomes for every event. The intercessor uses his position of grace and influence to lobby for God's very best outcome.

The principle is very clear. Any of us can intercede. Very few of us actually do.

The "take-home" principle here is that by God's grace toward us, we *can find favor* in His sight and *can intercede* with Him to achieve world-shaking results if we're willing to try.

In the New Testament

The first New Testament appearance of grace (finding favor) is in Luke 1:

> [26] And in the sixth month the angel Gabriel was sent from God unto a city of Galilee, named Nazareth, [27] To a virgin espoused to a man whose name was Joseph, of the house of David; and the virgin's name was Mary. [28] And the angel came in unto her, and said, Hail, thou that art highly favoured, the Lord is with thee: blessed art thou among women. [29] And when she saw him, she was troubled at his saying, and cast in her mind what manner of salutation this should be. [30] And the angel said unto her, Fear not, Mary: for thou hast found favour with God.

In this passage, it is clear that grace is flowing from the Greater to the lesser. Mary had *found favor* with God, and God gave her the most extravagant reward in history. She was permitted to carry the Lord Jesus in her womb from conception to birth. Mary was entrusted with the most sacred job of parenting in history, despite the hostility and gossip of disbelieving neighbors.

This is a marvelous example of God's grace. Mary obviously had pleased God in the past, and God knew she would put all her heart and soul into her ministry to Jesus. But Mary couldn't begin to *deserve* that honor. It was a gift from God.

The concept of grace next appears in the first chapter of the Gospel of John. Let's start with the context, verses 1–5:

> [1] In the beginning was the Word, and the Word was with God, and the Word was God. [2] The same was in the beginning with God. [3] All things were made by him; and without him was not any thing made that was made. [4] In him was life; and the life was the light of men. [5] And the light shineth in darkness; and the darkness comprehended it not.

Here we get a peek at the true nature of Jesus. He is God, and He created all things. He gave life to all creatures. He is described as light: the only ray of hope that we have in this dark world.

Notice verse 5: "And the light shineth in darkness; and the darkness comprehended it not." The word "comprehended" translates a compound

Durable Joy

Greek word *katalambano* meaning to seize eagerly. Jesus brought the light of His life into the world, to give us eternal hope. But we didn't eagerly seize it. We didn't get it. Many of us still don't get it very well, but God continues (for a little while longer) to make the light of Jesus available to us.

God's love and grace are very evident in verses 10 through 17:

> [10] He was in the world, and the world was made through Him, and the world did not know Him. [11] He came to His own, and His own did not receive Him. [12] But as many as received Him, to them He gave the right to become children of God, to those who believe in His name: [13] who were born, not of blood, nor of the will of the flesh, nor of the will of man, but of God. [14] And the Word became flesh and dwelt among us, and we beheld His glory, the glory as of the only begotten of the Father, full of grace and truth . . . [16] And of His fullness we have all received, and grace for grace. [17] For the law was given through Moses, but grace and truth came through Jesus Christ. (*NKJV*)

These verses absolutely take my breath away every time I read them. We humans are so out of contact with God that most of the folks in Jesus' day didn't recognize Him. God could have performed *justice* by vaporizing all the unbelievers on the planet after Jesus' crucifixion. But because of His *mercy*, He has reserved judgment for nearly 2,000 years.

Verse 12 is really amazing in its scope and simplicity, so let's read it again:

> [12] But as many as received Him, to them He gave the right to become children of God, to those who believe in His name. (*NKJV*)

Everybody who *receives* Him and *believes* (*trusts*) in Jesus' name qualifies for God's extravagant grace, and is permitted to be adopted as a child of God. The word "receives" translates the Greek word *lambano*, which can also be interpreted "gets it" or "understands."

It took me several months of study to "get it." It was hard to accept that trusting in the completed work of Jesus Christ qualifies us for eternal life and for an implant of God's own eternal nature in our hearts. This is pure grace.

Grace: The Big Loophole

This is the Big Loophole. This backwards principle is our key to surviving the spiritual warfare all around us and entering Heaven.

All God requires from us is a change of attitude and a willingness to submit. The Bible calls this repenting: turning *from* our old ways and turning *toward* Jesus, to follow Him. This tiny bit of effort enables us to *find favor* with God. Our faith—trusting in the completed redemptive work of Jesus Christ—qualifies us for God's extravagant grace.

This is pure grace, pure unmerited favor. If you think you *deserve* eternal life because of your natural goodness, then you still haven't received it. You still haven't repented of your self righteousness.

God's grace is the core principle of the Gospel message, in Romans 3, verses 23 and 24:

> [23] For all have sinned, and come short of the glory of God; [24] Being **justified freely by his grace** through the redemption that is in Christ Jesus.

Paul reinforces this principle in Romans 6, verse 23:

> For the wages of sin is death; but the **gift of God** is eternal life through Jesus Christ our Lord.

These verses changed my entire attitude toward God when I first read them. It was difficult to believe that I was a bad person, but easy to accept that I came short of God's standard of perfection, embodied in Jesus.

How do you compare to Jesus?

None of us come up to God's standard of perfection. In fact, Paul specifically deals with this issue in Romans 4, verses 4–8:

> [4] Now to him that worketh is the reward not reckoned of grace, but of debt. [5] But to him that worketh not, but believeth on him that justifieth the ungodly, his faith is counted for righteousness. [6] Even as David also describeth the blessedness of the man, unto whom God imputeth righteousness without works, [7] Saying, "Blessed are they whose iniquities are forgiven, and whose sins are covered. [8] "Blessed is the man to whom the Lord will not impute sin."

If you are less than Jesus in any respect, then your works come short of the glory of God, and you cannot earn Heaven on your own merits. This is not an insult, but a statement of fact.

In his letter to the Ephesians, chapter 2, verses 4–9, we see why we should be grateful for grace:

> [4] But God, who is rich in mercy, because of His great love with which He loved us, [5] even when we were dead in trespasses, made us alive together with Christ (by grace you have been saved), [6] and raised us up together, and made us sit together in the heavenly places in Christ Jesus, [7] that in the ages to come He might show the exceeding riches of His grace in His kindness toward us in Christ Jesus. [8] For by grace you have been saved through faith, and that not of yourselves; it is the gift of God, [9] not of works, lest anyone should boast. (*NKJV*)

Before we responded to the Gospel of grace, we were servants of sin, dead to the things of God. Now we are called to be dead to sin and servants of God.

What does it mean to "grow in grace?"

Good question. We find saving grace (favor) with God by responding in faith to the Gospel message. Then, out of a heart of gratitude to God, we seek to please God by doing more than the minimum required. God is God, and has all the power. He could demand perfect obedience, but knows we are not capable of it. His heart is responsive to the attitude of our hearts. It pleases God when we sincerely obey His commands and seek His face out of gratitude and faith in His Word.

The more we act in faith, the more blessings we will receive, both now and in Eternity. Sin, by definition, will pull us away from the center of God's will. Our short-sighted pleasure seeking can cost us untold blessings.

Jesus makes a precious offer in Matthew chapter 11, verses 28 to 30:

> [28] Come to Me, all you who labor and are heavy laden, and I will give you rest. [29] Take My yoke upon you and learn from Me, for I am gentle and lowly in heart, and you will find rest for your souls. [30] For My yoke is easy and My burden is light. (*NKJV*)

Jesus offers you *rest* from your religious burdens.

Jesus offers you His "yoke"—an opportunity to be a contributing member of His body here on earth. Jesus offers you a yoke of service that is easy and light compared to the bondage you formerly submitted to.

Jesus offers you the opportunity to spend time in fellowship with Him—He who is gentle and lowly in heart. Jesus offers you rest for your soul and durable joy in His presence.

The Real Confrontation

Before you can receive God's grace, you must confront the issue of your own sin. You must understand that all sin is horrible in God's eyes. If God didn't care about sin and its consequences, He would not have sent His Son to pay the price for sin on the cross at Calvary. If you could be saved by your own religious works, then Jesus was a fool for dying on your behalf. Hint: Jesus was not a fool.

All sin is punishable by eternal damnation in Hell. You have already committed sin. Your penalty awaits you. Somebody must pay the penalty for your sin, and you must decide who will pay. Will it be you or Jesus?

You can chose to serve your own sentence in Hell, and God will honor your choice. Or you can make a quality decision to submit to the Lordship of Jesus, and receive the gift of eternal life and your new born-again nature.

There are only two choices here. If there is a third choice, then God Himself is ignorant of it.

Receiving the Gift

Are you willing to receive His gracious gift? If so, take a moment and pray the simple prayer of faith that will enable you be born again and saved by God's grace:

The Prayer of Faith: Heavenly Father, I truly want to receive Your Son Jesus as my Lord and Savior. I confess that my best effort comes short of Your standards. I know that Jesus died a terrible death on a cross to pay the price for my salvation. I put my faith in Jesus's sacrifice for me, and repent of trying to earn Heaven by my own good works. Please send your Holy Spirit into my heart, to give me a new "born-again" nature, that I may life forever in Heaven with You. Fill me with your love and joy, that I find rest for my soul. I pray these things in Jesus' name, Amen.

If you prayed that prayer sincerely, your life will be different forever. If you prayed that prayer, the Holy Spirit now lives in your heart. The Holy Spirit will supernaturally enable you to understand the rest of this book.

If you can't bring yourself to pray the prayer quite yet, then fold down the corner of the page so you can find it quickly. Without the power of the Holy Spirit, you are helpless against the attacks of the enemy. Later, when you realize you can't make it on your own, you can return to this page, pray the prayer and begin your victorious new life.

Closing Prayer: Father, this is very strange to me. Help me to understand what your grace means for me, and how I can grow in the grace that you offer me. I pray this in Jesus' name. Amen.

Chapter 5

Faith

Be Sure of Your Salvation

Therefore, having been justified by faith, we have peace with God through our Lord Jesus Christ. *Romans 5:1 (NKJV)*

Opening prayer: Father, I want to spend eternity with You, in Your presence. Help me understand how to be sure of my salvation and walk in faith, I pray.

This chapter is about the ultimate "backwards" exercise: faith. Faith is completely contrary to human logic. Faith is putting complete confidence in the promises of an invisible God, despite the evidence of our worldly circumstances.

Faith is not a one-time backwards act. Faith is a lifelong process of trusting the promises of Scripture because we trust the One who makes the promises.

Faith is the process of following and trusting Jesus on the narrow path to Heaven. Faith calls us to distrust the pleas and taunts of folks on the well-worn path to destruction.

Faith is the backwards process of finding life through the merits of Jesus' death on the cross. Faith calls us to life by sending our fleshly lusts to the cross, despite their piteous cries for attention.

Faith enables us to find joy in the midst of hardship.

Faith sometimes requires heroic works, but the works themselves don't save us. To emphasize that point, let's look at Romans chapter 4, verses 1–3:

> [1] What then shall we say that Abraham our father has found according to the flesh? [2] For if Abraham was justified by works, he has something to boast about, but not before God. [3] For what does the Scripture say? "Abraham believed God, and it was accounted to him for righteousness." (*NKJV*)

When I was a little kid hearing Bible stories, guys like Abraham and David seemed like Supermen. They did lots of good deeds. But verses 1–3 make it clear that Abraham's good deeds didn't save him. Notice that "Abraham believed God . . ." (he acted in faith on what God said) ". . . and it was accounted to him for righteousness."

The word *accounted* translates a Greek business term *logizomai*, meaning to assign something (e.g. a payment or bonus or dividend) to somebody's account. Abraham didn't earn Heaven by attending 400 consecutive synagogue sessions, or reciting Torah verses, or by sacrificing oxen and sheep. Abraham pleased God by acting in faith on God's promise. As a result, God wrote "Paid in Full" on Abraham's ticket to Heaven.

We continue in Romans 4 with verses 4–8:

> [4] Now to him who works, the wages are not counted as grace but as debt. [5] But **to him who does not work** but believes on Him who justifies the ungodly, his faith is accounted for righteousness, [6] just as David also describes the blessedness of the man to whom God imputes righteousness apart from works: [7] "Blessed are those whose lawless deeds are forgiven, And whose sins are covered; [8] Blessed is the man to whom the Lord shall not impute sin." (*NKJV*)

According to verse 4, if we were capable of earning salvation by our works, then God would *owe* us something for doing all that religious stuff down here. Fortunately (or unfortunately, depending on how invested you are in religious stuff), God doesn't count our works. He counts our faith.

Note that in verse 5 we get the really Good News: "But to him who does not work but believes on Him who justifies the ungodly, his faith is accounted for righteousness."

Why does Paul keep repeating himself?

In Paul's day, most people didn't understand the concept of salvation by grace, bestowed freely on those who have faith. They still don't. For the first 30 years of my life, I never heard of the concept until I encountered the joyful people.

Even then, I fought the concept because it seemed so backwards. Could grace possibly be the secret of eternal life and durable joy? If so, why weren't more pastors preaching this?

It took several months of studying Scripture, but after reading and re-reading the book of Romans, I was convinced.

Now verses 9–10 of Romans chapter 4:

> [9] Does this blessedness then come upon the circumcised only, or upon the uncircumcised also? For we say that faith was accounted to Abraham for righteousness. [10] How then was it accounted? While he was circumcised, or uncircumcised? Not while circumcised, but while uncircumcised. *(NKJV)*

Let's pause for a second and let this point sink in. Abraham obeyed God in faith as a lifelong pattern. But his salvation was assured when he *began* acting in faith.

Are you ready for a lesson on Bible jargon? Our term for today is "the circumcision." In the Bible, it refers to the practice of the Law of Moses, symbolized by the mark of the circumcision on Hebrew men. Abraham underwent circumcision *as an act of faith* that God was able to keep His promise. The circumcision was the *outward sign* of Abraham's *inward faith*.

Circumcision did not save Abraham, any more than baptism can save you or your children. As we see in verses 11–12, the circumcision was merely an outward affirmation of his faith:

> [11] And he received the sign of circumcision, a seal of the righteousness of the faith which he had while still uncircumcised, that he might be the father of all those who believe, though they are uncircumcised, that righteousness might be imputed to them also, [12] and the father of circumcision to those who not only are of the circumcision, but who

also walk in the steps of the faith which our father Abraham had while still uncircumcised. *(NKJV)*

Remember the context. Paul's times were just like ours. Most of the pastors (rabbis) were infatuated by all the rules and regulations of the Law, rather than by God's call to faith. Then, as now, pastors (rabbis) found it easier to preach about sin rather than teach about faith. They trusted in their observance of the Law to earn them Heaven. God surely owed them an eternal debt of gratitude for all their tithes and all those Passover observances.

Paul had a notable religious career as a zealot for the circumcision. God personally ended Paul's religious career, and explained the way of salvation more clearly (see Acts, chapter 9). Paul thought he was perfectly righteous—until God struck him down. And Paul was fortunate that God didn't strike him dead.

What God showed Paul is that *nobody* is good enough.

Jesus astounded His disciples by saying that "unless your righteousness exceeds the righteousness of the scribes and Pharisees, you will not enter the Kingdom of Heaven." (Matthew 5:20) If *those* guys (advocates of the circumcision) weren't able to do enough good works, take a hint. Neither can we. Neither could Abraham, nor Paul.

Moving on to verses 13–16:

> 13 For the promise that he would be the heir of the world was not to Abraham or to his seed through the law, but through the righteousness of faith. 14 For if those who are of the law are heirs, faith is made void and the promise made of no effect, 15 because the law brings about wrath; for where there is no law there is no transgression. 16 Therefore it is of faith that it might be according to grace, so that the promise might be sure to all the seed, not only to those who are of the law, but also to those who are of the faith of Abraham, who is the father of us all. *(NKJV)*

To reinforce his earlier points, Paul repeats that the Law was given to the nation Israel *after* Abraham exercised faith in God's promises. That makes it clear that the promises derive from faith in God rather than from faith in the Law (i.e. in our own goodness and works).

To finish chapter 4, let's read verses 17–25:

[17] (as it is written, "I have made you a father of many nations") in the presence of Him whom he believed—God, who gives life to the dead and calls those things which do not exist as though they did; [18] who, contrary to hope, in hope believed, so that he became the father of many nations, according to what was spoken, "So shall your descendants be." [19] And not being weak in faith, he did not consider his own body, already dead (since he was about a hundred years old), and the deadness of Sarah's womb. [20] He did not waver at the promise of God through unbelief, but was strengthened in faith, giving glory to God, [21] and being fully convinced that what He had promised He was also able to perform. [22] And therefore "it was accounted to him for righteousness." [23] Now it was not written for his sake alone that it was imputed to him, [24] but also for us. It shall be imputed to us who believe in Him who raised up Jesus our Lord from the dead, [25] who was delivered up because of our offenses, and was raised because of our justification. (*NKJV*)

The story of Abraham is pretty remarkable. How many men would have the faith to undergo a painful surgery, at age 99, on the promise of having a natural son through a known-infertile 89-year-old woman?

Verses 19–21 are astonishing. Abraham did *not* waver at the promise of God through unbelief. He had faith. He gave glory to God. He was fully convinced that God was completely able and willing to keep His extravagant promises.

God counted *that* faith as righteousness. And—wonder of wonders—we can put our faith in the perfect work of Jesus and gain the same benefits of righteousness by faith.

God grits His teeth at my shortcomings, but He honors my faith. And He'll honor yours.

Salvation by faith *is* the Good News (Gospel) of Jesus Christ. We realize that we can be sure of our salvation, because it doesn't depend on our merits.

Amazingly enough, there's even more good stuff involved than inheriting Heaven at some unspecified future date. There are great benefits available now to believers.

In chapter 5, verses 1–4, Paul explains some of these benefits:

[1] Therefore, having been justified by faith, we have peace with God through our Lord Jesus Christ, [2] through whom also we have access by faith into this grace in which we stand, and rejoice in hope of the glory of God. [3] And not only that, but we also glory in tribulations,

knowing that tribulation produces perseverance; [4] and perseverance, character; and character, hope. (*NKJV*)

This is really great stuff:

- Faith gives us peace with God,

- Faith gives us personal access to God, and

- Faith gives us joyful hope of experiencing God's glory face-to-Face.

So why does Paul start talking about tribulation in verse 3? Isn't that the Bible word for trouble? How can Paul say we "glory in tribulations?"

Faith: The Secret of Durable Joy

Tribulation tests the genuineness of our faith and our joy. Furthermore, tribulation can even cause our joy to increase.

When we respond to hardship by trusting in God and praising Him, God strengthens our character. He builds endurance and hope and joy in our hearts. Nothing can shake our confidence in the faithfulness and integrity of our God. Therefore nothing can shake our confidence in our hope of eternal glory.

Now verses 5–8, one of the most amazing passages in the Bible:

[5] Now hope does not disappoint, because the love of God has been poured out in our hearts by the Holy Spirit who was given to us. [6] For when we were still without strength, in due time Christ died for the ungodly. [7] For scarcely for a righteous man will one die; yet perhaps for a good man someone would even dare to die. [8] But God demonstrates His own love toward us, in that while we were still sinners, Christ died for us. (*NKJV*)

Think about it. Now that you've begun trusting in the completed work of Christ, you've become a new person. God has actually begun changing your crusty old heart into something resembling His own. Most days, you're a decent person. In fact, you've been *really* good for several hours now.

But Jesus didn't die for you a few hours ago. He died for you before you permitted the Holy Spirit to begin cleaning you up.

Jesus died for the prisoner on Death Row, centuries before that prisoner repented of his sins.

Jesus died for the Apostle Paul, who wrote this epistle, while he was still known as Saul. Furthermore, Jesus not only forgave Saul for persecuting (murdering) His disciples, He permitted Saul/Paul to have an effective ministry that still benefits us today.

That type of love is too much for me to grasp. I'd be willing to lay down my life for my children, and you'd do the same for yours. But would I sacrifice my life to save a hardened murderer like Osama bin Laden or Charles Manson or Adolf Hitler? You probably wouldn't either.

Jesus willingly laid down His life for every sinner on earth, and thereby suffered the most painful death ever experienced.

Once this concept becomes real to you, you will never again doubt the character and faithfulness of God. Once you realize how God Himself suffered—for you—you will never again begin a sentence, "How could a good God . . ." Once you really grasp the awesome span of God's love, you'll never again doubt a single word of Scripture.

Verses 9–11 return to the subject of assurance of salvation:

> [9] Much more then, having now been justified by His blood, we shall be saved from wrath through Him. [10] For if when we were enemies we were reconciled to God through the death of His Son, much more, having been reconciled, we shall be saved by His life. [11] And not only that, but we also rejoice in God through our Lord Jesus Christ, through whom we have now received the reconciliation. (NKJV)

Face it: while you were still trying to *earn* your salvation, you were an enemy of God. You didn't feel like His enemy, but you were still in rebellion against His plan and His Son. Remember your attitude toward "those born-again religious" folk? Now you realize the cold fact: *you* were the religious one.

By repenting of your religious works and trusting in the merits of Jesus' perfect sacrifice, you became reconciled with God and set free from bondage to man-made religions.

Why am I making such a big deal of this? Because your salvation was and is a miracle. Being reconciled to God was impossible for the person that you formerly were. You were determined to do things your own way. Now, through your faith, you have become reconciled to God's way. You can be sure of your salvation.

Only *true* Christianity can promise you assurance of salvation. Only true Christianity bases your salvation on faith, rather than your religious performance or your *feelings* about your religious performance.

What must we do to *stay* saved?

The rules don't change after we come to Jesus. Faith in Him is all that can save us. Faith in His completed sacrifice is all that can keep us saved.

Some religions teach that you can lose your salvation at any time by committing certain sins. They (conveniently) also teach that you can regain your salvation by performing certain religious rituals. But these doctrines put too much reliance on the works of men and distract attention *away* from the completed work of Jesus.

Paul had strong words for the church in Galatia, where false teachers insisted that Christians must observe the Law of Moses in order to be saved. In Galatians 3, verses 1–3 we read:

> [1] O foolish Galatians! Who has bewitched you that you should not obey the truth, before whose eyes Jesus Christ was clearly portrayed among you as crucified? [2] This only I want to learn from you: Did you receive the Spirit by the works of the law, or by the hearing of faith? [3] Are you so foolish? Having begun in the Spirit, are you now being made perfect by the flesh? (NKJV)

In a future chapter on the Fruit of the Holy Spirit, we will see that God expects us to walk in our faith. If we walk with Him in faith, abiding in Jesus, allowing His Holy Spirit to change our hearts, our lives will bear fruit. We can truly experience His joy and peace in the midst of this world's turmoil and sorrow. We can have a personal relationship with the God of the universe, and walk in the assurance of our salvation.

What if I commit a mortal sin?

Scripture makes it clear that your faith, not your works, will determine your eternal destiny. Jesus already paid the price for you and every other person on earth. Nothing you can do can improve on the merits of His sacrifice or lessen its effectiveness.

Sin, however, can hinder your relationship with God and make it harder to hear His sweet voice in your prayers. Sin can steal your joy.

If you commit sin, confess it to God and restore your fellowship. Remember the promise in the first epistle of John, chapter 1, verse 9:

> [9] If we confess our sins, He is faithful and just to forgive us our sins and cleanse us from all unrighteousness.

The Christian's Bar of Soap

Sin can stain and harm you. Confessing your sin to God has two wonderful benefits:

- You receive judicial pardon for your sin. You are forgiven and escape the penalty of sin.

- Your heart and soul are purified from the effects of sin. This has profound implications for people who have been traumatized by assault or verbal abuse. Your initial injuries may have been caused by somebody else, but you allowed the enemy to build up a stronghold of bitterness and unforgiveness in your heart as a result. Confess *your* bitterness, and God will "cleanse you from all unrighteousness," including the wounds inflicted by the other person(s).

You can be sure of your salvation as long as you're trusting in Jesus and not in your own good works. Now that you're saved, you can concentrate on pleasing Him by walking in faith. You don't need to fret about your future. Just follow Jesus.

The book of Hebrews makes it clear that Jesus' redemptive work on your behalf is completely finished, as we see in chapter 7, verses 24–27:

[24] But He, because He continues forever, has an unchangeable priesthood. [25] Therefore He is also able to save to the uttermost those who come to God through Him, since He always lives to make intercession for them. [26] For such a High Priest was fitting for us, who is holy, harmless, undefiled, separate from sinners, and has become higher than the heavens; [27] who does not need daily, as those high priests, to offer up sacrifices, first for His own sins and then for the people's, for this He did once for all when He offered up Himself. (*NKJV*)

That is the Lord that I serve. Jesus loved me enough to pay a terrible price for my salvation. I can trust a Lord like Him more than I can trust my own works.

Closing Prayer: Lord, thank You for paying such a price to save a religious fool like me. Lord, I put my trust completely in the merits of Your perfect sacrifice. Thank You for cleansing me, reconciling me and giving me assurance of my eternal future. Amen.

Chapter 6

Baptisms

"Into what, then, were you baptized?"

He said to them, "Did you receive the Holy Spirit when you became believers?" They answered him, "We have never even heard that there is a Holy Spirit." *Acts 19:2*

Opening prayer: Father, there is a lot of misunderstanding about baptisms. Please open our hearts to understand both water baptism and being baptized with the Holy Spirit, we pray in Jesus' name.

When we were kids, we used to enjoy bending the rules. It was a fun game to see how much we could get away with. It didn't seem like much fun if we had to be completely obedient to our parents.

Durable joy comes from a completely different source. Durable joy comes from acting in faith on God's word in Scripture, even if it seems peculiar or unpleasant to do so.

The next few chapters will help you understand subjects that often puzzle and trouble new believers. These subjects *must* be important to your joy, because the devil has inspired centuries of conflict and confusion around them.

The first of these subjects is baptism. Most people are familiar with the concept of water baptism, but there's another baptism that can bring even more joy to a believer, as we shall see.

Good Intentions Don't Count

The apostle Paul met folks in Ephesus that *thought* they were Christians but didn't have a clue. We read the beginning of the story in Acts 19:

> [1] And it happened, while Apollos was at Corinth, that Paul, having passed through the upper regions, came to Ephesus. And finding some disciples [2] he said to them, "Did you receive the Holy Spirit when you believed?" So they said to him, "We have not so much as heard whether there is a Holy Spirit." [3] And he said to them, "Into what then were you baptized?" So they said, "Into John's baptism." *(NKJV)*

This little group apparently had sincerity and faithfulness, since they were observing *something* besides the local flavor of idolatry. They might have even called themselves disciples of Jesus. But the Holy Spirit gave Paul the discernment that they were missing something.

Getting it right

Paul took three steps to get the Ephesians on the right track:

- He explained the plan of salvation more clearly, as we have done in the preceding chapters of this book.

- He explained the proper meaning of water baptism. This is implied by the fact that they wanted to be baptized in water again.

- He introduced and explained the concept of being baptized with the Holy Spirit.

Water Baptism

Our word *baptism* translates the Greek word *baptisma*, which means *dipping* or *immersion*. It is related to another Greek word *baptismos*, which refers to ceremonial washings performed by Jewish people.

John the Baptist taught baptism (*baptisma*) as a symbol of repentance from sin. Later, the disciples of Jesus taught baptism as a symbol of identification with their Lord.

The symbolism of Christian water baptism is very simple. When a person is lowered under the water, the picture is that of a person dying or drowning voluntarily, without putting up a struggle. When the new believer is lifted back above the surface of the water, it is a picture of being raised from the dead by God's power.

The obvious parallel is to the death, burial and resurrection of Jesus. Jesus permitted the Roman soldiers to take His life, and His lifeless body was laid into an underground tomb. Three days later, God raised the body of Jesus to life.

When we are baptized, we declare that we're voluntarily dying to our old way of ignorance and spiritual death. We thereby identify with our Lord, who died for us. We confess that our old life (our old religion) was powerless to save us, and we willingly give it up.

When we're lifted to the surface, we declare that by trusting in God's power and grace, we will be raised to walk in newness of life.

You *should* be baptized in water

Jesus voluntarily submitted to be baptized by John the Baptist, not to earn His salvation but to serve as an example for us. You should be baptized in water as a sign to the outside world that you are a born-again believer in Jesus Christ. You should be baptized as an act of obedience to the commands of Jesus.

In the last two verses of the gospel of Matthew, chapter 28, verses 19–20 we read:

> [19] Go ye, therefore, and teach all nations, baptizing them in the name of the Father, and of the Son, and of the Holy Spirit, [20] teaching them to observe all things whatsoever I have commanded you, and lo, I am with you always, even unto the end of the world. Amen.

This is clear and simple. Jesus is *not* describing the plan of salvation. He is telling the disciples to go and teach other people to follow Jesus. People who follow Jesus *should* do certain things as an act of faith in the principles shown in Scripture.

Does water baptism save you?

At Calvary, one of the two criminals crucified with Jesus repented and gave his heart to Jesus before he died. Jesus said to him, "Today thou shalt be with me in paradise." (Luke 23:43) Nobody took that criminal down from the cross and baptized him before he died. But he had Jesus' personal assurance that he would instantly go to Heaven on his death.

Most of us have a bit more available time than the criminal on the cross. We can surely find time, between now and the grave, to obey a simple request of Jesus.

Some denominations teach that baptism—*in accordance with their rules and doctrine*—is required for salvation. Don't believe it. If you study the Scriptures for yourself, you might discover that these same denominations deviate from Scripture in some of their other doctrines, too.

Infant Baptism

Only one group of people ever got baptized in the Bible: those old enough to make a conscious decision to follow the Lord. Baptism was (and should be) an act of obedience performed *after* a person begins to trust in Jesus.

Infant baptism is a meaningless religious ritual in God's eyes. The baby is too young to make a conscious decision to follow Jesus. It's as pointless as trying to *wish* salvation on a stubborn sinner.

On the other hand, many churches perform Baby Dedications. The parents bring their young ones forward for the pastor and congregation to pray over them. In this way, the parents dedicate themselves to raising the children to follow Jesus, in accordance with the Scriptures.

If you were baptized as an infant, please don't be angry if your pastor suggests getting baptized to celebrate your new birth in Jesus. If you rebel against this simple command of Jesus, then ask yourself "Why not?" It's just part of growing up. You should make a public identification with the death, burial and resurrection of your Lord. Receive water baptism, so you can move on to the more exciting baptism: being baptized with the Holy Spirit.

Immersed in the Holy Spirit

The people that Paul encountered *said* they were disciples of John the Baptist. They had been baptized in water as a symbol of their repentance from sin. But they very likely were converted and baptized secondhand, by traveling disciples of John. Their ignorance of the Holy

Spirit was not John's fault. John's teaching concerning baptism and the Holy Spirit is featured prominently in all four Gospels.

Let's start with Matthew chapter 3, verses 11–12:

> ¹¹ "I indeed baptize you with water unto repentance, but He who is coming after me is mightier than I, whose sandals I am not worthy to carry. **He will baptize you with the Holy Spirit and fire.** ¹² His winnowing fan is in His hand, and He will thoroughly clean out His threshing floor, and gather His wheat into the barn; but He will burn up the chaff with unquenchable fire." *(NKJV)*

These verses introduce the concept of Holy Spirit baptism as well as the fire of judgment. Jesus will baptize His people with the Holy Spirit and gather them like wheat into His barn. Those who rebel against His Holy Spirit will be torched. It's a simple black-and-white choice. There will be no half-burned weeds in Heaven, and no half-toasted wheat grains from Purgatory.

We see the same message in the Gospel of Mark, chapter 1, verses 7–8:

> ⁷ And he preached, saying, "There comes One after me who is mightier than I, whose sandal strap I am not worthy to stoop down and loose. ⁸ I indeed baptized you with water, but **He will baptize you with the Holy Spirit.**" *(NKJV)*

In Luke 3:16–17, we see the same message:

> ¹⁶ John answered, saying to all, "I indeed baptize you with water; but One mightier than I is coming, whose sandal strap I am not worthy to loose. **He will baptize you with the Holy Spirit and fire.** ¹⁷ His winnowing fan is in His hand, and He will thoroughly clean out His threshing floor, and gather the wheat into His barn; but the chaff He will burn with unquenchable fire." *(NKJV)*

This account is very similar to the one in Matthew, with its reminder that not everything growing in the Lord's field is real wheat.

The Gospel of John, chapter 1 verses 32–33 has a slightly different perspective, quoting John the Baptist *after* he had baptized Jesus in the Jordan:

³² And John bore witness, saying, "I saw the Spirit descending from Heaven like a dove, and He remained upon Him. ⁻³³ "I did not know Him, but He who sent me to baptize with water said to me, 'Upon whom you see the Spirit descending, and remaining on Him, **this is He who baptizes with the Holy Spirit.**'" *(NKJV)*

When you see the Gospel accounts side-by-side, several points jump out at you:

- This must be an important subject, to be mentioned in *all four* Gospel accounts.
- John the Baptist taught this on multiple occasions, both before and after he had baptized Jesus in the Jordan River.
- The precise phrase is being "baptized with the Holy Spirit."
- The baptism with the Holy Spirit is an essential part of the Christian experience. Like water baptism, it is *not* an absolute requirement for salvation. However, like water baptism, it is a matter of obedience. If you rebel against either type of baptism, maybe you aren't really saved.

As we saw earlier, the word baptism means dipping, used in the Greek language to describe the process of dying a garment or drawing water from a pot. To be baptized with the Holy Spirit means to be immersed in God and brought up filled or drenched in Him.

This is a very precious offer from God. The Creator of the universe is willing to immerse you in Himself. The implications are staggering. To refuse this precious offer ("My denomination says that stuff is from the devil.") is to insult the One who created you, and to risk being left behind on the threshing floor.

If you have been innocently ignorant of this baptism, please keep reading. The Lord has a very special treat for you.

Jesus also spoke of the baptism of the Holy Spirit, in Acts chapter 1, verses 4–8:

⁴ And being assembled together with them, He commanded them not to depart from Jerusalem, but to wait for the Promise of the Father, "which," He said, "you have heard from Me; ⁵ for John truly baptized with water, but **you shall be baptized with the Holy Spirit** not many days from now." ⁶ Therefore, when they had come together, they asked Him, saying, "Lord, will You at this time restore the kingdom to Is-

rael?" [7] And He said to them, "It is not for you to know times or seasons which the Father has put in His own authority. [8] "But **you shall receive power when the Holy Spirit has come upon you**; and you shall be witnesses to Me in Jerusalem, and in all Judea and Samaria, and to the end of the earth." (*NKJV*)

This passage gives us even more insight:

- This was our Lord's final conversation with His disciples before ascending to Heaven.

- The disciples' minds were cluttered with ambitious notions and questions about Jesus' Kingdom. Jesus brushed all that aside to focus their attention on their upcoming baptism with the Holy Spirit.

- Jesus commanded the disciples *not* to begin their evangelistic work until *after* receiving this baptism.

- The disciples were already saved. They had trusted in Jesus for their salvation and had been baptized in water.

- The disciples were already trained. They had been personally tutored by Jesus for three years. They had already made missionary trips, preaching the Gospel. They had worked powerful miracles and cast out demons in Jesus' name.

- The disciples were saved, water baptized, trained, sincere and enthusiastic. They had already achieved certain things in Jesus' name. But they had not yet received *power*.

You might be saved, water baptized, trained, sincere and enthusiastic. Perhaps you have already achieved certain things in Jesus' name. But until you have been baptized with the Holy Spirit, you have not received the *power* that Jesus considered essential.

Until you receive this *power*, you will be trying to do the work of God in your own strength. God may bless you partially, but the fullness will elude you.

The very first Baptism with the Holy Spirit was not subtle, as we see in Acts 2:

[2] And suddenly there came a sound from Heaven, as of a rushing mighty wind, and it filled the whole house where they were sitting. [3] Then there appeared to them divided tongues, as of fire, and one sat upon

each of them. ⁴ And they were all filled with the Holy Spirit and began to speak with other tongues, as the Spirit gave them utterance. *(NKJV)*

This was different than anything the disciples had ever experienced before. In fact, it's probably different from anything that *you* have ever experienced.

Wasn't this a one-time event, never to be repeated?

That is true. However, special outward manifestations of God's power accompanied several events in the Book of Acts. One notable event was Acts 4, verses 29 through 31:

> ²⁹ "Now, Lord, look on their threats, and grant to Your servants that with all boldness they may speak Your word, ³⁰ "by stretching out Your hand to heal, and that signs and wonders may be done through the name of Your holy Servant Jesus." ³¹ And when they had prayed, the place where they were assembled together was shaken; and they were all filled with the Holy Spirit, and they spoke the word of God with boldness. *(NKJV)*

The disciples were praying for boldness, because they were beginning to encounter opposition. The disciples had great faith, and they were praying for God to keep His promises (always a good idea). God sent a tiny manifestation of His power to shake the building, and sent a mighty manifestation of His power to give His people boldness.

Another special event is in Acts 10, verses 44–47:

> ⁴⁴ While Peter was still speaking these words, the Holy Spirit fell upon all those who heard the word. ⁴⁵ And those of the circumcision who believed were astonished, as many as came with Peter, because the gift of the Holy Spirit had been poured out on the Gentiles also. ⁴⁶ For they heard them speak with tongues and magnify God. Then Peter answered, ⁴⁷ "Can anyone forbid water, that these should not be baptized who have received the Holy Spirit just as we have?" *(NKJV)*

Peter was preaching the Gospel to Gentiles who feared the God of Israel but were not born Jewish. As Peter spoke, they believed his message and began trusting Jesus for their salvation. In response to their faith, God sent the Holy Spirit upon them in great power. The believers who were "of the circumcision" were astonished because the Gentiles had: ". . . received the Holy Spirit just as we have."

A third special event is in Acts 18:25–26.

> [18] But at midnight Paul and Silas were praying and singing hymns to God, and the prisoners were listening to them. [26] Suddenly there was a great earthquake, so that the foundations of the prison were shaken; and immediately all the doors were opened and everyone's chains were loosed. *(NKJV)*

Wait a minute! None of these events happened just like Acts chapter 2.

That's exactly my point. God often manifests His miraculous power for a special occasion. But He never allows Himself to be put into a ritualistic pattern.

God does this for a reason. In the five books of Moses, God precisely spelled out important worship procedures. He called for special types of sacrifices to be performed by specially dedicated priests on specially designated occasions in a specially designed Tabernacle. He did this for a reason: to point *forward* to His Son, Jesus, the Messiah of Israel. All the rituals and Tabernacle furniture painted a picture of Jesus, so we would be sure to recognize Him when He came. Only the Messiah could fulfill *every* symbol of Tabernacle worship.

In the New Testament, Jesus came and perfectly fulfilled the prophecies. The Mosaic Law and Levitical worship procedures are now like maps in a museum. They still paint an accurate picture, but we no longer put our trust in them. The Messiah has already come. Now we put our trust in Him.

Under the New Covenant, Jesus says, "Follow Me." If we obediently follow Jesus and become baptized with the Holy Spirit, God Himself comes to dwell in our hearts. If we submit to the Holy Spirit and walk uprightly, He will transform our lives from the inside out.

If we continue steadfastly walking in faith, submitted to the Holy Spirit, we become a functional part of the Body of Christ, the Church, with Jesus Himself as our Head. This composite picture, then, will look like Jesus. Individually we still have good days and bad days, but we still have a role to play in His body.

The net effect is that when a non-believer encounters the Church, he or she should encounter Jesus. The Holy Spirit will work through us to speak to that person's heart. From time to time, the Holy Spirit may require a miracle to be done through our hands or through our prayers.

If we are functioning parts of Christ's body, miracles should be a normal part of our lives.

Many denominations teach that the Baptism of the Holy Spirit happens at the same time as conversion. They think *all* believers are baptized with the Holy Spirit automatically.

There is a grain of truth in that. All believers *do* receive the Holy Spirit in their hearts at the moment of conversion. That's what it means to be born again: to be given a supernatural implant of God's own nature within us. The Lord's disciples were saved. They were born again, and had an implant of God's Holy Spirit in their hearts. But until Pentecost, they were not yet empowered for service.

Empowered for Service

A passage in Acts 8 illustrates this principle:

> [5] Then Philip went down to the city of Samaria and preached Christ to them. [6] And the multitudes with one accord heeded the things spoken by Philip, hearing and seeing the miracles which he did. [7] For unclean spirits, crying with a loud voice, came out of many who were possessed; and many who were paralyzed and lame were healed. [8] And there was great joy in that city. [9] But there was a certain man called Simon, who previously practiced sorcery in the city and astonished the people of Samaria, claiming that he was someone great, [10] to whom they all gave heed, from the least to the greatest, saying, "This man is the great power of God." [11] And they heeded him because he had astonished them with his sorceries for a long time. [12] But when they believed Philip as he preached the things concerning the kingdom of God and the name of Jesus Christ, both men and women were baptized. [13] Then Simon himself also believed; and when he was baptized he continued with Philip, and was amazed, seeing the miracles and signs which were done. *(NKJV)*

Make no mistake about it: God was working powerfully through Philip. People were repenting of their sins and being baptized. The sick were healed. Demons were cast out. "And there was great joy in that city" (verse 8). Even the local sorceror was impressed. God was working mighty things—*through Philip*. But there's more to the story:

> [14] Now when the apostles who were at Jerusalem heard that Samaria had received the word of God, they sent Peter and John to them, [15] who, when they had come down, prayed for them that they might

receive the Holy Spirit. [16] For as yet He had fallen upon none of them. They had only been baptized in the name of the Lord Jesus. [17] Then they laid hands on them, and they received the Holy Spirit. (NKJV)

We learn quite a bit from this story:

- There was nothing wrong with the work that Philip had done. God had used him mightily to accomplish His will.

- The people of Samaria were genuinely saved and water-baptized before being baptized with the Holy Spirit.

- The joy they felt was genuine, and proof that the Holy Spirit had already begun working in their hearts.

- The miracles were done by Philip, who *had* received the Baptism of the Holy Spirit.

We are *not* told why Philip didn't pray for them to receive the Holy Spirit. My personal conjecture is that God deliberately worked this way to illustrate a principle: that the indwelling of the Holy Spirit is separate from the infilling of the Holy Spirit in power.

So what happens when people become baptized with the Holy Spirit?

Good question! We've already seen some examples in the Book of Acts. At Pentecost, the disciples miraculously spoke in other languages, so that all the foreigners in Jerusalem observing the feast were able to hear in their own languages. At other times, people spoke in unknown tongues or began to prophesy. Sometimes there were miracles and healings. In every case, the believers seemed to have a different type of experience.

Despite the diversity of experiences, we can generalize that the baptism with the Holy Spirit does two things to the believer:

- The believer receives spiritual *gifts*.

- The believer begins to bear spiritual *fruit*.

Both the gifts and the fruit of the Holy Spirit are profound subjects, discussed in later chapters of this book.

Now let's return to our original story in Acts 19 and read verses 4–6:

> [4] Then Paul said, "John indeed baptized with a baptism of repentance, saying to the people that they should believe on Him who would come after him, that is, on Christ Jesus." [5] When they heard this, they were baptized in the name of the Lord Jesus. [6] And when Paul had laid hands on them, the Holy Spirit came upon them, and they spoke with tongues and prophesied. (*NKJV*)

What should strike you about this scene is how *normal* it is. You can see these activities (conversion, water baptism, laying on of hands, and Holy Spirit gifts) on a regular basis in a good, Bible-believing church.

This was a small group of people, and the display of the Holy Spirit's power didn't shake the ground or part the river in the middle. And it's clear that Paul and the other early believers believed the infilling with the Holy Spirit and the gifts were a separate transaction from salvation and water baptism.

What's the formula for getting baptized with the Holy Spirit?

In our Scriptural examples, we saw believers receive the Baptism several different ways:

- The disciples at Pentecost received the Holy Spirit by praying as a group as commanded by Jesus. They had been specifically promised this baptism by Jesus, and were acting in faith, expecting to receive it.

- The Gentiles at Cornelius' house received the Holy Spirit while Peter was still explaining the basic Gospel message to them. They had no expectation of this baptism, but God blessed them with it for His glory and for our education.

- The believers in Samaria received were baptized with the Holy Spirit when Peter and John laid hands on them and prayed for them. This appears to be the most-common method in Scripture.

A few friends of mine (actually, only two, and they live in opposite ends of the country) received the baptism with the Holy Spirit almost by accident, like the people in Cornelius' house. Both were members of churches that taught against the Holy Spirit gifts. Both began speaking in tongues spontaneously, without any effort or expectation. One was just a teenager at the time. This type of baptism *might* happen to you, but don't hold your breath.

At various times in Church history, groups of believers (from non-Spirit-filled denominations) have sparked revivals by gathering together to pray persistently for the infilling of the Holy Spirit. These Christians just *knew* that God wanted to baptize them with the Holy Spirit, and were determined to pray until they received that blessing.

In my personal experience, the surest way to be baptized with the Holy Spirit is to find a good Bible-believing, Spirit-filled congregation and have a responsible person (pastor, counselor, home group leader, deacon, or elder) pray with you.

I tried that, but I haven't experienced anything special yet!

Not everybody has an "experience" at the time. As a home group leader and counselor, I've seen the full range of possibilities:

- Some have felt a peaceful joy come over them, moving them to tears.

- Some have immediately begun speaking in tongues.

- Some (very few) have passed out.

- One fellow (at an outdoor evangelistic crusade) prayed with us to receive Jesus as Lord and Savior, and asked for the Holy Spirit baptism—anything that might help him get free of drugs. As we prayed, he passed out and lay on the ground—twitching occasionally—as we continued praying over him for release from the demons that had run his life. When this man finally came to his senses 15 minutes later, his first words were: "What was *that?*" We explained that the Holy Spirit had immersed him, filled him, and done a healing work in his heart—under a general anesthetic. The experience was dramatic and real, but rare.

- Some other people haven't felt anything at the time. Your teacher was in this group. That's a story to be told in another chapter.

If you have not yet received the baptism of the Holy Spirit, you have a wonderful experience ahead of you. If your church congregation teaches *against* the baptism with the Holy Spirit, ask God to lead you to another congregation. If you aren't sure where to look or what to look for, try finding the nearest Calvary Chapel.

The next step

Once you have received the baptism with the Holy Spirit, you are uniquely equipped for two very peculiar activities:

- As you receive the **gifts of the Holy Spirit**, you will be empowered to work miracles in God's service, to help build up the body of Christ.

- As the indwelling Holy Spirit works in your heart, you will begin bearing **the fruit of the Holy Spirit**—the distinctive character traits of our Lord Jesus. Then you will begin to experience the durable joy that God promises to those who believe in Him.

Bearing the fruit of the Holy Spirit is much more important than operating in the gifts of the Holy Spirit. Character change is a greater miracle than a medical healing. Character change makes the power and love of Jesus Christ seem real to nonbelievers. Character change is unmistakable proof that God takes a personal interest in every sinner who repents and follows Jesus.

Turn the page and learn more.

Closing Prayer: Lord, I earnestly desire *all* that You have for me, even if it sounds a little strange to me at first. Fill me with Your Spirit, and guide me in Your truth, I pray in Jesus' name, Amen.

Chapter 7

Fruit of the Holy Spirit

Durable Joy and More

"But the fruit of the Spirit is: love, joy, peace, long-suffering, kindness, goodness, faith, meekness, self-control." *Galatians 5:22–23*

Opening Prayer: Father, I know that Your Holy Spirit is willing and able to bear fruit in my life. Please help me to become more fruitful, I pray.

*E*ven in this computerized world, we all understand the concept behind fruit trees. The farmer plants seeds in prepared soil, and nurtures the trees to maturity. Then, for a period of years, the farmer is able to harvest crops of fruit from these mature trees.

God uses this familiar concept to illustrate how we should live. He plants *some* type of seed in our hearts and obtains *some* type of harvest. In the rest of this lesson, we will explore both the seed and the resulting fruit crop.

Before you can bear the fruit of the Spirit, you must first have the life of the Spirit. The preceding chapters have carefully explained how the seed (the Scriptures—the Word of God) can be planted in your heart to give you eternal life.

Jesus described this in Matthew 13:

> [3] Then He spoke many things to them in parables, saying: "Behold, a sower went out to sow. [4] "And as he sowed, some seed fell by the wayside; and the birds came and devoured them. [5] "Some fell on stony places, where they did not have much earth; and they immediately sprang up because they had no depth of earth. [6] "But when the sun was up they were scorched, and because they had no root they withered away. [7] "And some fell among thorns, and the thorns sprang up and choked them. [8] "But others fell on good ground and yielded a crop: some a hundredfold, some sixty, some thirty." (*NKJV*)

Which one of these represents you?

- If your heart is hardened to the Gospel, then the seed of the Scripture never has a chance to take root in your heart. Barring a radical change, you will die a bitter, hardened person and spend eternity in Hell.

- The second part of the parable is easy to understand, but very sad. At one point in your life, perhaps in your school years, you recognized the truth of the Gospel and had a temporary, superficial response to it. But as the years went by, you found other treasures to occupy your heart and mind. Now there's no trace of your initial enthusiasm, and the Gospel is a distant childhood memory. You are not necessarily a "bad" person, but you are essentially a dead person. If you return to Jesus with all your heart, you can recapture the joy and live with Him eternally. Otherwise, you may spend eternity in Hell.

- The third part of the parable is familiar to us, and is also sad. Perhaps you came to the Lord at a Harvest Crusade or a Billy Graham meeting, and have been attending church more-or-less regularly since then. But your heart and mind are very full of other stuff. You admire the people who intimately know the Scriptures, and perhaps have read parts of the Bible. But the Lord Jesus Christ is not the ruling passion in your life. "Maybe someday" you'll take a class or something. You are saved (I hope), but your life is not bearing any fruit helpful to others.

- The fourth part is my favorite. Regardless of when you received and responded to the seed of the Word, you have made a conscious decision to make Jesus the Lord of your life. You have given the Holy Spirit permission to rule your heart and change it from the inside out. The Holy Spirit, in turn, has made your life fruitful. Maybe you wasted 10 or 20 or 30 years of your life following other priorities. But *now* you are living a mature commitment to Jesus, and your life is a fruitful blessing to those around you.

Which of these apply to you? Are you a fruitful blessing to your Christian brothers and sisters?

Don't kid yourself that it's too late for your life to make a difference for the Lord. You might have wasted more years than most. But the God that raised Jesus' body from the grave can change your heart, *if you submit to Him*. On the other hand, if the ruling passion in your life is to remain a stubborn fool, God will respect your decision.

You needn't worry about catching up to anybody else. The minute you submit to the Lordship of Jesus, you are just where the Lord wants you to be. Now let's look at some practical steps to help you become fruitful.

Understanding Fruit

First of all, recognize that your life is already bearing *some* type of fruit all the time. You have no choice in the matter. It's how God designed you. The key is ensuring that you bear the right type of fruit.

God introduces the concept of bearing fruit in the very first chapter of the Bible, in Genesis 1, verses 11–12:

> [11] Then God said, "Let the earth bring forth grass, the herb that yields seed, and the fruit tree that yields fruit according to its kind, whose seed is in itself, on the earth;" and it was so. [12] And the earth brought forth grass, the herb that yields seed according to its kind, and the tree that yields fruit, whose seed is in itself according to its kind. And God saw that it was good. *(NKJV)*

There are several important points in these two simple verses:

- Some plants are like grains and grasses. If cultivated, a portion of the crop must be held back as seed for the next year's harvest.

The plants themselves die out after the growing season. These crops must be planted, cultivated, harvested, and replanted in an annual cycle.

- The planting, cultivating, harvesting and replanting of grains and grasses are a picture of Christian service. We must continually do certain types of work: evangelizing, helping the needy, participating in missions activities, serving in child care, teaching Bible classes, etc. The gifts of the Holy Spirit are given to enable us to do these works. **The gifts of the Holy Spirit empower us for service.** You can jump in and start productively serving as soon as you become Spirit-filled. These gifts will be described in the next chapter.

- **Fruit trees are a picture of your heart**. It can take years for a Christian to reach maturity and bear the fruit of the Holy Spirit.

- **The fruit of the Holy Spirit is a changed heart.** A heart changed by the Holy Spirit has the attributes mentioned above in Galatians 5:22–23: Love, joy, peace, long-suffering, kindness, goodness, faith, meekness, self-control.

- Note what God teaches us about seeds: every herb "yields seed according to its kind." Likewise every fruit tree "yields fruit according to its kind, whose seed is in itself." **Every plant yields seeds according to its kind**. Jesus said a tree is known by its fruit, whether good or bad. You can't harvest figs from thorn bushes.

- **You are continually reproducing what is in your heart,** whether good or bad. If your heart is a thorn bush, it is yielding a continual harvest of thorns and seeds without your conscious knowledge or control.

The good news is that you are not a helpless spectator in this process:

- Your conscious decision to receive the free gift of salvation by faith enabled you to receive an implant of eternal life in your heart.

- By receiving and exercising the gifts of the Holy Spirit, you permit God to work powerfully through you in His service.

- Your ongoing submission to the Lordship of Jesus Christ enables the Holy Spirit to nourish this new nature and bring it to fruit-bearing maturity.

Psalm 1 clearly describes the importance of making good choices:

[1] Blessed is the man who walks not in the counsel of the ungodly, nor stands in the path of sinners, nor sits in the seat of the scornful. [2] But his delight is in the law of the Lord, and in His law he meditates day and night. [3] He shall be like a tree planted by the rivers of water, that brings forth its fruit in its season, whose leaf also shall not wither; and whatever he does shall prosper. *(NKJV)*

The first good choice is to reject the bad counsel, the bad habits and the scornful attitude of people who don't know God. This isn't rocket science. You already know the individuals in your life who continually sow the weed seeds of bitterness. Don't be a weed eater.

The second good choice is to get good input. Delight yourself in the Scriptures. When I first started out, reading the Bible was like taking medicine. I had to proceed in faith, trusting God to keep the promise that in His presence is fullness of joy. Within a few weeks, reading the Bible at lunch was more fun than joining the guys playing cards. God *gave* me delight in studying Scriptures. That was a miracle. God can do the same for you.

The third good choice is to be consistent. Verse 3 says, "And in His law he meditates day and night." The word "meditate" in the Hebrew means to walk around muttering things under your breath continually. Memorize certain key verses. Repeat them to yourself. Spend time morning and night feeding your heart with Scripture.

The fourth good choice—implied but not specifically mentioned in Psalm 1—is to obey the leading of the Holy Spirit. As you make daily choices to avoid the bad and to feed on Scripture, the Holy Spirit will give you "nudges" every now and then. He will call you to acts of obedience, to be undertaken in faith. He might call you to give up a favorite bad habit or to start attending a mid-week Bible study or an early-morning prayer meeting. Every time you obey His leading, He will bless you and give you even greater joy in your walk.

If you concentrate on these four things, your heart will automatically begin bearing fruit. You don't have to grimace into the mirror and tell yourself to be fruitful. The Holy Spirit is already at work, digging out weeds and cultivating the seed of the Word that you've been planting in your heart.

Not just for pastors

Don't be intimidated and think the gifts and fruit of the Holy Spirit are just for full-time ministers. This is basic stuff. Jesus, Himself, makes it clear that bearing fruit is the distinctive characteristic of being a Christian.

Let's read John 15, verses 1–3:

> [1] "I am the true vine, and My Father is the vinedresser. [2] "Every branch in Me that does not bear fruit He takes away; and every branch that bears fruit He prunes, that it may bear more fruit. [3] "You are already clean because of the word which I have spoken to you." (*NKJV*)

These are familiar verses, surely. But you must not miss the profound truth within them:

- Jesus takes the concept of fruit-bearing very personally. He considers *Himself* to be the vine or tree, and He considers us (you and me) to be His branches. That is an intimate connection.

- Jesus *expects* all of us to bear fruit, so it must be very do-able.

- It is normal for a branch to bear fruit if it is receiving nourishment from the vine. If you and I are *not* bearing fruit, then our connection to the Vine is suspect.

- If you and I are *not* bearing the fruit of the Holy Spirit in our lives, we run the risk of being taken away and burned . . . somewhere. Remember the *second* type of seed planting mentioned earlier? Take a hint.

- You must expect some pruning to take place in your life. Anybody who has raised fruit trees knows that limbs would break under the weight if every single fruit bud were allowed to grow to maturity.

- Although the disciples had not consciously been aware of it, Jesus had already been cleaning (pruning) the disciples through His teachings. He had already taken away some of their foolish notions of grandeur and self-importance. Before long, the disciples would experience further purging and cleansing.

Some of the Lord's early pruning might be transparent and painless to us. Yet our family and friends will notice the difference in our lives. More on this subject later.

The Meaning of Life

Take a deep breath and read verses 4 through 6, three of the most important verses in the Bible:

> [4] "Abide in Me, and I in you. As the branch cannot bear fruit of itself, unless it abides in the vine, neither can you, unless you abide in Me. [5] "I am the vine, you are the branches. He who abides in Me, and I in him, bears much fruit; for without Me you can do nothing. [6] "If anyone does not abide in Me, he is cast out as a branch and is withered; and they gather them and throw them into the fire, and they are burned." (*NKJV*)

Jesus has just told you the meaning of life.

- **Abiding in Jesus must be the central fact of your life**. This is not a mystical, mysterious concept. It's very simple. Abiding (the Greek word *meno*) is the common word for staying somewhere. You might *visit* the grocery store, but you *abide* in your home. You spend quality time there. It is important to you.

- **Abiding in Jesus is the key to bearing fruit**. You must be connected to Him, through the ministry of the Holy Spirit, like a branch to its vine.

- **Abiding in Jesus means spending quality time with Him**. The Gospel of John, chapter 1, verse 14 says, "The Word was made flesh, and dwelt among us." We can no longer see His fleshly body, but we can spend quality time in the Scriptures, the written Word. And we can have quality fellowship with Jesus through prayer, praise, and worship (singing).

- **Abiding in Jesus means having fellowship with other believers**. Since Pentecost, the church has been the body of Christ. He is our head. We are members of His body through the ministry of the Holy Spirit. If you are *not* regularly attending a Bible-believing fellowship, you are not receiving proper nourishment. If you are *not* in accountable relationship to other believers, you are not properly connected to the Vine. "He who has ears, let him hear what the Spirit says to the Churches." For more information on this subject, see the chapter "B-Team" later in this book.

- **Jesus wants to have daily fellowship with you.** He wants to bear *much* fruit in your heart and life. He wants to give you the joy that comes from being in His presence. He wants you to walk in power and love and joy, making His love real for people around you—people who might go to Hell unless somebody shares Jesus with them.

- **You can't do this in your own strength.** Your heart is too corrupt and deceitful without the life-changing power of the Holy Spirit.

- **The alternative to abiding in Jesus is abiding in Hell.** Don't let the warm-fuzzy-minded people confuse you. Either Jesus was a liar, or He is God in the flesh. If Jesus is God, and if verse 6 is true, then we must organize our life's priorities around abiding in Him.

A changed heart's desire

Are you ready for another shock? Let's read verse 7:

⁷ "If you abide in Me, and My words abide in you, you will ask what you desire, and it shall be done for you." *(NKJV)*

This is simply astonishing. Can it possibly be true? Up to this point, I was already prepared to abide in Jesus—just because it's the *right* thing to do. Now Jesus makes this extravagant promise.

Note the scope and key of this promise. The scope of the promise is unlimited. The key is the quality of the abiding.

If we are daily engaged in filling our hearts and minds with Scripture, and *if* we are daily seeking the Lord and His face, the Holy Spirit is at work in our hearts. Over time, the Holy Spirit changes our hearts.

As we die to our own selfish agendas, we begin to feel the Lord's heart. As we learn to move in response to the Holy Spirit's tender leadings, we become better connected to Jesus, our Head. As we become better connected to our Head, we begin wanting what He wants.

When we reach the point in our lives where we can truly say, "Thy will be done," then we will experience the truth of verse 7. When we know the heart of God, we can pray confidently for His will to be done. When we pray for His will, His own power energizes our lives and our prayers. His will *shall* be done, when you abide in Him and delight to do His will.

Will *you* believe this promise from the Lord? Are *you* willing to yield your will and your plans to God and seek His will and His plans? If so, then "miracles" will become a normal part of your walk with Him.

Miracles? Through me? How?

Very simple. God's nature and His will haven't changed since Jesus' day. Likewise, human nature and needs haven't changed since Jesus' day. Yielded vessels, faithful in their abiding, will constantly be directed by God to touch human needs in Jesus' name. The only limitation is in your willingness and faithfulness in the abiding.

Let's continue with verse 8:

> 8 "By this My Father is glorified, that you bear much fruit; so you will be My disciples." (*NKJV*)

Don't let the glittering promise of miracles distract you from God's central purpose. He wants you to abide in Jesus and bear the fruit of a changed life.

Sometimes we pray for a miracle of healing, in hopes it might help unbelievers turn to the Lord. This is an unrealistic prayer. Jesus performed astonishing miracles of healing, but the hard-hearted people weren't moved by it. Most of the crowd was just there to be entertained and maybe fed with free loaves and fishes. Miracles don't touch hard hearts.

Likewise Christians sometimes pray for gifts of the Spirit so they can be impressive evangelists or preachers or teachers. "Maybe," they reason, "I can reach more people if I can become an eloquent preacher/ teacher!" The apostles were eloquent preachers (and miracle workers), but they were whipped, beaten and stoned by the very people they were trying to help. Eloquent preaching doesn't touch hard hearts.

This verse says that the best way to touch hard hearts is to demonstrate the fruit of the Holy Spirit in your life. Your family *noticed* the difference in your character after you began spending quality time in Scripture and prayer. They might not *like* the difference, but they must give God the glory for His life-changing power.

- When a hard heart becomes tender by the power of the Spirit, God is glorified.

- When a workaholic husband becomes a loving, attentive spouse, God is glorified.

- When a frenzied career woman becomes a calm, loving wife and mom again, God is glorified.

- When a rebellious, angry young man turns from drugs and becomes a loving son, God is glorified.

- When a hardened prison inmate becomes a real, caring person through the working of the Holy Spirit, God is glorified.

These aren't the only Scriptures on this subject. Jesus began His ministry by reading from the prophet Isaiah. Let's read chapter 61, verses 1–3:

> [1] "The Spirit of the Lord GOD is upon Me, because the LORD has anointed Me to preach good tidings to the poor; He has sent Me to heal the brokenhearted, to proclaim liberty to the captives, and the opening of the prison to those who are bound; [2] To proclaim the acceptable year of the LORD, and the day of vengeance of our God; to comfort all who mourn, [3] To console those who mourn in Zion, to give them beauty for ashes, the oil of joy for mourning, the garment of praise for the spirit of heaviness; that they may be called trees of righteousness, the planting of the LORD, that He may be glorified." *(NKJV)*

Jesus stopped reading in the middle of verse 2 because the remainder of the passage was still future on *that* day. The "day of vengeance" is still future, as is the consolation of Zion in verse 3.

However, since Pentecost believers in Jesus have been able to experience "The Spirit of the Lord GOD is upon me." Since Pentecost, believers have experienced the blessings of verse 3:

- Consolation of those who mourn,

- Beauty for ashes,

- The oil of joy for mourning,

- The garment of praise for the spirit of heaviness,

- Being fruitful trees of righteousness, the planting of the Lord, and

- God has been glorified because of the fruitfulness of believers.

When we bear much fruit, through the work of the abiding Holy Spirit, God is glorified.

Let's finish with verses 9 through 14 of John 15:

> [9] "As the Father loved Me, I also have loved you; abide in My love. [10] "If you keep My commandments, you will abide in My love, just as I have kept My Father's commandments and abide in His love. [11] "These things I have spoken to you, that My joy may remain in you, and that your joy may be full. [12] "This is My commandment, that you love one another as I have loved you. [13] "Greater love has no one than this, than to lay down one's life for his friends. [14] "You are My friends if you do whatever I command you." (NKJV)

Do you *really* love Jesus? Does it show in your love for your brothers and sisters in Christ? Does it show in your love for unlovely and unlovable people?

Remember the context of this passage. Jesus had just washed 12 pairs of feet. He was careful to wash the feet of Judas, knowing that Judas would soon leave to betray Him. Then He said that we must follow His example in ministry.

Admit it: this is really difficult. Your God-given gift of discernment tells you that the person in front of you is a weasel or maybe just a plain waste of time. But the Holy Spirit tells you to minister to that person anyway. Because if we don't minister to a Judas every once in awhile, then maybe we're not really ministering much at all.

This is too difficult to do in your own strength. The Holy Spirit must first change your heart, and bring forth fruit in response to your faithful abiding in Jesus.

Is your fruit ripe or rotten?

Have you noticed that ripe fruit doesn't stay fresh forever? If not consumed, it will rot.

The Holy Spirit can bear wonderful fruit in our lives, but it is perishable. If we get complacent in our walk and start admiring the work that God has done, we stop bearing fresh fruit. Before long, we smell funny.

God painted a picture of this in Exodus chapter 16:

> [4] Then said the LORD unto Moses, Behold, I will rain bread from heaven for you; and the people shall go out and gather a certain rate every day, that I may prove them, whether they will walk in My law, or no.

The children of Israel were commanded to go out and gather manna every morning except the Sabbath. They were to keep nothing as leftovers, except on the day before the Sabbath. Any leftover manna became wormy and rotten the second day, except on the Sabbath.

The fruit of the Holy Spirit is a miracle of God, and the Lord can use the fruit of our lives to nourish our families and acquaintances. But we can never become complacent and pronounce ourselves complete and perfect in character.

We must seek God and abide in Him every morning. We must gather fresh manna and bear fresh fruit in our lives every day.

In conclusion . . .

If you truly love Jesus, you *will* keep His commandment and *will* abide in His love, seeking Him faithfully every morning. Then you *will* bear *much* fruit of the Spirit in your heart. And your joy will be full, as King David describes in Psalm 16:

> [8] I have set the LORD always before me: because He is at my right hand, I shall not be moved. [9] Therefore my heart is glad, and my glory rejoiceth: my flesh also shall rest in hope . . . [11] Thou wilt show me the path of life. In Thy presence *is* fulness of joy; at Thy right hand there are pleasures for evermore.

> **Closing Prayer:** Father, as I seek to abide in the presence of Your Son, Jesus, change my heart to love what You love. Give me durable joy in your presence as I seek to do your will. Make me a vessel of Your love, that Your name may be glorify ed in all that I do, I pray in Jesus' name, Amen.

Chapter 8

Gifts of the Holy Spirit

His Body Building

Now concerning spiritual gifts, brethren, I do not want you to be ignorant. *1 Corinthians 12:1*

Opening prayer: Father, how should I view the gifts of Your Holy Spirit, and how can I know which ones are for me? Please help me understand Your plan to equip me for service. Amen.

The gifts of the Holy Spirit are essential to the Christian walk. Their operation was key to the growth and survival of the early Church. Their operation is still essential to the growth and survival of the present-day Church. The present-day Church is dysfunctional to the extent that it misunderstands and wrongly applies these precious gifts.

This is not a "fringe" subject. The gifts of the Holy Spirit are not luxurious items that are attained only by pastors or some religious elite. Nor are they merely "soldier" weapons, used only by the warrior class.

God Himself gives us these gifts. They are essential to building up His Church. We cannot do any part of God's work unless we are exercising these gifts and manifesting the fruit of the Holy Spirit in our lives.

Once a person has been baptized with the Holy Spirit, as described in the "Baptisms" chapter, he or she will start becoming a different person. This will happen in two different ways:

- As the believer makes daily conscious choices to submit to the gentle leading of the indwelling Holy Spirit, the believer's character is changed. The resulting **new character traits** are called "The Fruit of the Spirit"—subject of the previous chapter in this book.

- The Holy Spirit will empower the believer with **new abilities**, called "The Gifts of the Holy Spirit." These gifts enable the believer to do the Lord's work in new (and sometimes miraculous) ways. Think of them as "birthday gifts" in honor of our new birth.

Let's begin by reading from Paul's first letter to the Corinthians, chapter 12, verses 1 through 3:

> [1] Now concerning spiritual gifts, brethren, I do not want you to be ignorant: [2] You know that you were Gentiles, carried away to these dumb idols, however you were led. [3] Therefore I make known to you that no one speaking by the Spirit of God calls Jesus accursed, and no one can say that Jesus is Lord except by the Holy Spirit. *(NKJV)*

Verses 2–3 don't appear to concern spiritual gifts, but they do. Paul is warning that there are religious charlatans both inside and outside the church. The "Christian" charlatans mislead people by appearing to operate in the Holy Spirit gifts. Some of the charlatans even say, "Jesus is Lord," in an attempt to sound Scriptural.

But Paul wasn't talking about the mere words "Jesus is Lord." In his day, the residents of the Roman empire were required to proclaim, "Caesar is Lord" on demand, to show their loyalty to Caesar. To say "Jesus is Lord" was to sign their own death warrant. *That* type of sincerity only comes when a believer is moved and empowered by the Holy Spirit. How many of the TV-only "ministers" have that type of sincerity?

Necessary Diversity

In the next four verses, Paul lays down some important principles:

[4] There are diversities of gifts, but the same Spirit. [5] There are differences of ministries, but the same Lord. [6] And there are diversities of activities, but it is the same God who works all in all. [7] But the manifestation of the Spirit is given to each one for the profit of all. (*NKJV*)

At first glance, Paul appears to be repeating himself. But there are some keen distinctions to be made here:

- Verse 4 tells us that there are **different gifts** given to different people. If all the people in a group are operating in different gifts in submission to the Holy Spirit, there will be a supernatural harmony and peace despite their diversity.

- Verse 5 emphasizes that God calls different people to **different categories of ministry**. Most of us are not called to be ordained ministers of the gospel. However, all of us are called to minister to the needs of those around us. We are all called to share the Good News of Jesus Christ.

- Verse 6 tells us that even within similar ministries, the Holy Spirit leads different ministers to perform **different activities**. Not all evangelists are on TV. Not all have open-air stadium ministries. Not all teachers are pastors, and not all pastors are gifted as teachers.

- Verse 7 is the summary. God gives different gifts to each person individually, but **He wants the gifts to benefit His people as a group**. Properly used, the gifts of the Holy Spirit will inevitably build up the body of Christ, the Church. Selfishly used, the gifts of the Holy Spirit don't help anybody.

In verses 8–10, Paul gives us a partial listing of the gifts:

[8] For to one is given the word of wisdom through the Spirit, to another the word of knowledge through the same Spirit, [9] to another faith by the same Spirit, to another gifts of healings by the same Spirit, [10] to another the working of miracles, to another prophecy, to another discerning of spirits, to another different kinds of tongues, to another the interpretation of tongues. (*NKJV*)

Notice that in this first grouping, Paul lists the gifts without explaining them. This implies that his readers were quite familiar with the gifts. They had either personally experienced or seen these gifts on a daily basis.

But what *are* these gifts?

In general, these are distinctive gifts conveyed by the Holy Spirit to the believer. They involve spiritual power working through a human agent. These gifts are given *after* the recipient becomes a born-again believer. Before you came to the Lord, did you walk around discerning spirits or miraculously healing your friends? Were you born speaking prophetically for God? I didn't think so.

Please note that these are not enhanced versions of the natural gifts that God bestowed upon you at birth. Your natural gifts may include musical talent, verbal skills or athletic abilities. After you come to the Lord, the Holy Spirit may enable you to use your natural talents in a ministry context. But natural gifts are quite different from spiritual gifts.

You've probably noticed that the devil has cheap imitations of these powers, but they surely aren't "gifts." The enemy of your soul dangles spiritual power as bait, to entrap the foolish. There's a huge difference between Spirit-gifted believers and demon-possessed persons. Unfortunately, many of the latter group actively pretend to be the former. More on that subject later.

Let's go through Paul's first list.

Word of Wisdom

Wisdom is simply applied knowledge. We experience the word of wisdom when the Holy Spirit gives us supernatural wisdom in a particular situation. If you are a Spirit-filled believer, you might have already experienced this gift:

- In your daily walk, the Holy Spirit will sometimes empower you to share the Gospel with another person. The Holy Spirit will miraculously give you words to touch the heart of that person. When it happens, you *know* that your intellect didn't concoct that word of wisdom. It came from the heart of God, as a gift to that soon-to-be believer.

- If you regularly study Scripture, the Lord will often illuminate your understanding, and show you how to apply the Word during the day. The word of wisdom will always help one or more believers and thereby edify (build up) the Body of Christ.

The word of wisdom is not a flashy gift, and the charlatans don't mimic this during their fund-raising campaigns. But it comes first on God's list for good reason. Godly wisdom is essential to your walk with God. Consider these words from Proverbs chapter 3:

> [13] Happy is the man who finds wisdom, and the man who gains understanding; [14] For her proceeds are better than the profits of silver, and her gain than fine gold. [15] She is more precious than rubies, and all the things you may desire cannot compare with her. [16] Length of days is in her right hand, in her left hand riches and honor. [17] Her ways are ways of pleasantness, and all her paths are peace. [18] She is a tree of life to those who take hold of her, and happy are all who retain her. (*NKJV*)

Think about it. Wisdom is a profound gift from the Lord, and one that He delights to give us, if we diligently seek it.

If wisdom from God can bring happiness, long life, riches, honor and peace, we can stop right here and be content. But God has other gifts to bestow.

Word of Knowledge

Sometimes the Holy Spirit reveals something that the believer couldn't possibly have known otherwise. In Acts chapter 5, for example, the Holy Spirit told Peter that Ananias was lying.

Sometimes in your prayer times, the Lord will reveal something to you. Maybe that word is for you, to encourage you or convict you of a particular sin.

On rare occasions, the word is for (or about) somebody else or some group. In any case, the Holy Spirit bestows these words of knowledge to accomplish His own purposes.

Please exercise great wisdom concerning the word of knowledge. If someone gives you "a word from the Lord," you must evaluate that word in the light of Scripture and in the context of what you *know* God is doing in your life.

By the same token, don't be offended if you share a word of knowledge with somebody and that person doesn't immediately take action. Sure, *you* believe it's from the Lord, but the Holy Spirit and Scripture must make that word real for the intended recipient.

The word of knowledge is not God's answer to the Psychic Hotline. When you receive such a word, immediately ask the Lord for wisdom in how to apply it.

Faith

God loves to see us exercise faith in Him. He grants us eternal salvation when we exercise faith in the redeeming sacrifice of His Son, Jesus, rather than in our own righteousness. Without faith it is impossible to please God (Hebrews 11:6), so faith must be as natural for the Christian as breathing.

This faith is something special. At specific times, God gives us clear directions to step out in faith in a particular situation, and the results are often miraculous (at least in our eyes).

We exercise faith when God's promises are more real to us than our circumstances. We exercise faith when we act on the basis of God's will, as revealed in Scripture and confirmed by the Holy Spirit.

An important principle is shown in Romans 10:17:

 17 So then faith cometh by hearing, and hearing by the word of God.

The word of God is revealed to us in two ways. There is Scripture (the Greek word *logas*), which shows us God's general will. There are also times when the Holy Spirit quickens a particular Scripture or otherwise gives us a word (the Greek word *rhema*) concerning God's specific will in *this* situation. The passage above uses the word *rhema*, meaning that faith is when we respond to the Holy Spirit's specific guidance.

In the book of Judges, chapter 6, the Holy Spirit came upon Gideon. Then the Lord directed Gideon to act in faith to defeat an opposing army of about 130,000 Mideonites (Judges chapter 7). God told Gideon to send 99% of his army home, so that Gideon's band of 300 men could defeat the enemy simply on the basis of God's power. Gideon did, and God did.

The boy David acted in faith on the Scriptures, facing the giant Goliath. David didn't trudge forward speaking dull religious platitudes. David shouted out praises for the power and glory of the God of Israel. Then he ran to what appeared to be certain death at the hands of the Philistine. God knew differently. David's faith overcame his circumstances.

If you read the book of Acts, you'll find dozens of examples where disciples acted in faith on God's Scriptures and in response to the direct leading of the Holy Spirit. These days, we have a lot more Scripture than the early disciples. More of God's will has been written down and published for all to see. But that doesn't free us from the responsibility of asking God to guide us in situations where His will isn't perfectly clear.

Gifts of Healings

Notice that the Bible talks about Gifts (plural) of Healings (also plural). These are individual packages of healings given to specific persons. Your friend next door may receive healing from a cancerous condition, or somebody in New York may receive a healing for a chronic kidney problem. These are gifts to the specific persons, from God.

Healings are a very precious gift from God. All sickness comes as a result of Adam's fall, as the wages of sin. Therefore a healing is more than a welcome relief from suffering. It is a miraculous, partial reversal of The Curse. Each healing is a special act of God's love in our behalf.

God is willing to bestow a gift of healing through the prayers of *any* Spirit-filled Christian, assuming a healing is God's will for the recipient.

Some believers are greatly used by God as a conduit for His healing gifts. In most cases, these believers are successful in their prayers because they are good listeners. They pray to hear the will of God first. Then they can pray with 100% confidence because they are lined up with God's will in that situation.

That's why I don't speak about individuals having "The Gift of Healing." That puts the emphasis on the brother or sister doing the praying, rather than on God or the recipient of the gift of healing. I'd rather say that brother or sister has "The Gift of *Hearing*"—a special case of the Word of Knowledge discussed earlier.

". . . to another the working of miracles . . ."

Let's stop here and compare God's plan to our weak flesh (human) nature. God wants to give us the gifts in a deliberate sequence. He wants us to receive Wisdom, Knowledge and Faith before we start praying for healings or other miracles.

Unfortunately, human nature is foolish, ignorant, faithless and impatient. We like the easy way, the convenient way, the spectacular way. We want to jump in and start praying for great riches or spectacular miracles before growing in spiritual maturity.

God's plan is better. He wants us to enter His Kingdom as little children: with enormous capacity to learn and grow, but limited power and authority at first. As a 12-year-old boy with big feet, I was repeatedly told I would "grow into" the feet. Likewise, God will enable us to "grow into" full operation in His gifts.

It takes a lot of Wisdom and Faith to discern God's will for a miracle. But if we are abiding in Christ and faithfully studying Scripture, the Holy Spirit will show us His will. Just don't be surprised (or impressed with yourself) when He asks you to work a miracle. The Lord will occasionally ask you to pray for a miracle. Miracles should be a normal part of our walk. We should always have our hearts tuned to hear God's voice, just in case.

Will God work miracles through me?

Maybe, but not necessarily. Most of the time, the work of the Holy Spirit is quiet and hidden. Most of His work involves changing our hearts and character to be useful to Him.

You wouldn't dream of letting a child play with a loaded gun. A wise parent first instructs the child over time before trusting him or her to act responsibly with a powerful weapon. Likewise the Holy Spirit seeks to change our hearts, to make us more like our Lord, before entrusting us with great power.

". . . to another prophecy . . ."

God's prophets work two ways. Most of the time, they speak forth God's will in accordance with Scripture. At certain times, they will foretell future events.

In real life, prophecy works like a combination of the Word of Wisdom and Faith. The prophet operates in the Lord's wisdom, and speaks in faith in obedience to the Holy Spirit.

Some characteristics of prophets:

- God's prophets always seek to glorify God. They trust God in every circumstance, and delight to declare His faithfulness to His Word.

- God's prophets always seek to know God's will through Scripture. Their hearts are prepared by diligent study.

- God's prophets always seek to edify other believers. As Jesus said, "Freely you have received; freely give."

- God's prophets always speak according to the will of God, consistent with Scriptures.

- God's prophets always speak the truth, and their predictions are 100% accurate. In the Law of Moses, just *one* wrong prediction was enough to qualify a person for stoning. Today's prophets would walk more humbly if that rule still applied.

If somebody claims to be a prophet but consistently falls short in these areas, he or she is a false prophet, a wolf looking for weak sheep. Such a person is *not* a brother or sister in Christ and must be quickly removed from your fellowship. Don't even eat lunch with him/her.

On the other hand, some well-intentioned Christians think they've heard from the Lord on certain subjects, and make silly predictions about the future. Their behavior brings dishonor upon God and His church. Forgive them, but bring the wrong predictions to their attention in a loving way, just as you would for any other type of sin or shortcoming. The Holy Spirit will guide you and give you wisdom, if you ask Him.

". . . to another discerning of spirits . . ."

To be honest, most believers are a little bit uncomfortable with this gift. We don't want to know how many demons are floating around out there. It sounds pretty scary.

Fortunately, God doesn't ask us to go around counting demons. But there are specific times when we absolutely *must* know the truth of a particular situation. For example, we must know:

- **Whether a person's words and actions are motivated by the Holy Spirit, by a demon, or by that person's own flesh nature.** Pastors, in particular, must constantly exercise this discernment. Likewise, you and I must exercise discernment concerning our pastors and teachers. You should pray for discernment about this book. And you must really pray for discernment when you are around people operating in the Spirit gifts; the enemy is always seeking to infiltrate our home groups and prayer groups. Even right-on teachers and pastors have bad days and crappy messages. Your discernment will enable you to know whether their teaching is demonic or just uninspired. Likewise, some really "off-center" teachers can seem to have right-on messages. Nothing wrong with their words. The gift of discernment will enable you to know God's opinion, and will alert you to the little clues of demonic influence.

- **When a demonic spirit is operating in a particular situation.** Wake up, believers! When you feel down and depressed shortly after a major accomplishment for the Lord, wake up! It might be an attack from the enemy (revenge). Then, too, it might be plain old fatigue. Either way, you're very vulnerable when you're tired. Get "covering" prayer from your spouse, pastor or from a strong believer of the same gender. Let that person break the grip of the enemy and pray some steel into your shield. If you're in a tough situation and not sure of your discernment, you probably *are* under attack and should call for help. Remember: religious spirits love to operate in churches. The first instance of Jesus casting out a demon was in a synagogue. I've personally observed demonic powers operating in *all* types of churches, from mainline denominational to wild-side splinter groups. Even in very good church fellowships, a particular meeting can suffer a heavy lifelessness until somebody exercises discernment and prays (usually silently) to break it. One morning, I was guest-teaching a Sunday-morning Bible class at a Presbyterian church and was surprised at the silent heaviness over everybody at the beginning. A few minutes later I discerned the spiritual oppression and said a quick, silent prayer. The spirit immediately broke and fled, and the group became its usual cheerful gathering.

- **When a particular person is demon-possessed.** Most of the time, this will be obvious to a Spirit-filled believer. Instantly start praying for the Holy Spirit to give you wisdom to know God's will in that situation. Be careful to do nothing more or less than God's will, even if God's will is to walk away. And have faith that what God requires, He enables. The tricky part is that "possession" is often a part-time situation, triggered by drinking or drugs. Years ago, a short, soft-voiced woman in our apartment complex became a raging monster during a drinking bout. She began throwing living room furniture through her front window, screaming profanity in a voice not her own. Before and after this event, she was congenial, educated and articulate. Without discernment, you would *never* have believed the story from any of the witnesses.

Does the content of this section shock you? Just remember Paul's words in Ephesians chapter 6, verses 12–18:

[12] For **we do not wrestle against flesh and blood**, but against principalities, against powers, against the rulers of the darkness of this age, against spiritual hosts of wickedness in the heavenly places. [13] Therefore **take up the whole armor of God**, that you may be able to withstand in the evil day, and having done all, to stand. [14] Stand therefore, having girded your waist with truth, having put on the breastplate of righteousness, [15] and having shod your feet with the preparation of the gospel of peace; [16] above all, taking the shield of faith with which you will be able to quench all the fiery darts of the wicked one. [17] And take the helmet of salvation, and the sword of the Spirit, which is the word of God; [18] praying always with all prayer and supplication in the Spirit, **being watchful** to this end with all perseverance and supplication for all the saints. *(NKJV)*

According to this passage, God requires us to recognize the spiritual nature of our daily walk. We're in a battle, and you can't see the enemy. Therefore we must *be* watchful (verse 18) with our supernatural senses, exercising discernment along with the gifts of wisdom, knowledge and faith.

. . . to another different kinds of tongues, to another the interpretation of tongues.

The "different kinds of tongues" is a peculiar gift. The most-famous example was when the 120 disciples began speaking in other tongues on the Day of Pentecost. God chose this day and this particular miracle to spread His gospel as rapidly as possible. Pentecost was a pilgrimage day, and devout Jews from everywhere were in town to observe the feast. Each of the pilgrims heard the disciples proclaim the Gospel of Jesus Christ *in his own language.*

Just as each gift of healing is a partial reversal of the general curse on humanity, the gift of tongues on that occasion was a partial reversal of the curse and confounding of languages at Babel. While the Pentecost-style miracle of tongues may have been repeated elsewhere, we have no record of it in Scripture.

In later passages in the Book of Acts, different groups of disciples spoke in tongues unknown both to themselves and their hearers. For example, before Peter could finish sharing the Gospel message with the Gentiles in Cornelius' house, the Holy Spirit fell upon these Gentiles and they began speaking in other tongues. To fully appreciate how odd this miracle was, consider the Scriptural pattern for believers up to that time:

- An unbelieving person hears the Gospel message and decides to become a believer.

- The formerly unbelieving person makes a profession of faith to begin trusting in the completed work of Jesus. At that moment, the Holy Spirit takes up residence in the heart of the believer to perform His precious work of salvation and transformation.

- As an outward demonstration of his inward profession, the new believer gets baptized in water.

- At some point, perhaps at the first profession of faith or perhaps years later, the new believer prays to receive the baptism with the Holy Spirit, as described in the earlier chapter on Baptisms. Frequently, this will involve another believer praying for and laying hands upon the new believer.

- After the baptism with the Holy Spirit, the gifts of the Spirit will begin to appear.

The above is not the only way it can happen, but it had already become a tradition in the early church. Furthermore, the Apostles had only been sharing the Gospel with Jewish people and occasional Samaritans.

What's so wrong with that?

God didn't want the church of Jesus Christ to become a Jewish sect. He wanted all men, everywhere, to hear the Gospel message and live forever. The Holy Spirit acted to shake the Apostles out of their newly formed comfort zone.

The Holy Spirit made it clear to Peter that Gentiles could be converted and Spirit-filled exactly like Jewish believers. To drive home His point, the Holy Spirit came upon the people of Cornelius' house in a way that looked backwards to Peter.

These days, the gift of tongues is sometimes called "prayer language." It is a wonderful way to praise and worship the Lord in our private devotions.

In public worship gatherings, the gift of tongues poses a problem. With rare exceptions, nobody understands what is being spoken in the prayer language. It sounds like utter foolishness. It can easily be faked. Even when genuine, it can be an irritating distraction. Worse, it makes unbelievers (and new believers) very uncomfortable.

The gift of tongues is a major issue that the church must confront squarely. The gift must be very important, or the devil wouldn't spend so much time generating confusion and counterfeits. To ensure that we get it right, we will describe tongues in greater detail in a later chapter.

Before we end our discussion of individual gifts, let's talk briefly about certain odd types of behavior that pretend to be inspired by the Holy Spirit.

The "Gift of Foolishness"

From time to time, groups gain notoriety by promoting activities not described in Scripture: hysterical laughter, growling like lions and barking like dogs. These practices don't glorify God. Barking doesn't lead sinners to Jesus. Hysterical laughter doesn't offer the water of the Holy Spirit to souls thirsty for God.

Don't be led astray by the spiritual-sounding foolishness that some folks indulge in. Almighty God, Creator of the Universe, does not appreciate being blamed for their silliness. The Holy Spirit sometimes makes believers do surprising things, but you can bet He never makes people act foolish in front of TV cameras. To the best of my knowledge, there is no Gift of Foolishness. Foolishness is the opposite of Wisdom, which does come from God. Ordinary human flesh (and demons) can look plenty foolish without any help from God, thank you.

Jesus didn't act like that. Jesus arose up before dawn to pray in private. Then He quietly walked in the power of God, preaching the gospel, healing the sick and delivering sinners from death. Enough said.

In Conclusion

As we said before, God gives gifts to build up His Church, the body of Jesus Christ. They may seem odd from a human perspective, but God has both a Plan and a Problem, as we'll see in the upcoming chapter titled "B-Team."

Closing Prayer: Heavenly Father, I'm so grateful for the gifts You have given me through, Your Holy Spirit. Please give me wisdom and grace to use these gifts for Your glory, and to build up my brothers and sisters in Christ, Amen.

Chapter 9

The Whole Armor of God

Making Your Joy Durable

Why, LORD, do you stand at a distance and pay no heed to these troubled times? Arrogant scoundrels pursue the poor; they trap them by their cunning schemes. The wicked even boast of their greed; these robbers curse and scorn the LORD. In their insolence the wicked boast: "God doesn't care, doesn't even exist." *Psalm 10:1–4, NAB*

Opening Prayer: Heavenly Father, there are times when I just can't understand how this world has gotten so crazy, and why the trend is worse instead of better. Help me see the world from Your perspective, and recognize the survival tools that You have created for my benefit, I pray. Amen.

So far in this book, we have discovered how God can give us joy through the operation of His Holy Spirit in our hearts. The question now is whether God's joy can be durable enough to survive enemy attacks.

Face it: life doesn't make sense at times. It feels like we're under attack from all directions at once. There are warped people everywhere, abusing drugs, abusing alcohol, abusing each other, and planning ways to abuse you.

Why do people act that way? It's not rational. Thirty years ago, my college professors taught, with religious fervor, that human beings are basically good and will behave rationally when provided with the proper education and economic incentives.

If they were right, there should be relatively few irrational people these days, because knowledge is so widespread and cheap, and psychology has had more than 100 years to help man perfect himself.

Unfortunately, education has not made the bad guys into nice people. It has made them craftier and wealthier.

Who is the real enemy?

In the aftermath of the September 11 tragedy, the television commentators spent endless hours coming to grips with the magnitude of the attack and the bizarre nature of the terrorists involved. To paraphrase one frustrated newsman:

"How can you protect yourself against an enemy that hides himself, pretends he doesn't exist, masks his activities behind a smokescreen of innocent civilians, maintains an army of spies and undercover agents, hates you with an irrational hatred and will try to attack you at any opportunity?"

The newsman was speaking of the terrorists behind the September 11 attacks. But his description perfectly fits a different type of enemy, the real enemy responsible for all the unrest in this world.

- Our real enemy is not radical Islam, although the real enemy has been able to use the Islamic militant groups to do his bidding.

- Our real enemy is *not* communism, although the real enemy has used communism to enslave billions and murder millions of people.

- Our real enemy is *not* secular humanism, although humanism has become the politically correct religion of our government and educational system.

- Our real enemy is *not* the popular news media, although some commentators speak with his voice.

- Our real enemy is *not* a religious myth, although he has instigated all the religious foolishness that has plagued mankind since Adam and Eve.

The apostle Paul describes the real enemy very succinctly in his letter to the Ephesians, chapter 6:

> [12] For we do not wrestle against flesh and blood, but against principalities, against powers, against the rulers of the darkness of this age, against spiritual wickedness in high places. *(NKJV)*

Paul, writing under the inspiration of the Holy Spirit, says that we shouldn't waste time complaining about our visible enemies. Our real enemy is the devil, Satan himself, supported by an invisible army of demon spirits and their hierarchy of regional commanders.

Your politicians can't legislate these creatures away. The FBI can't tap their phones or monitor their e-mails. Your door locks won't keep them out of your home. Your dog can't bite them. Your "nice" behavior won't prevent them from attacking you and your family.

Good news: You can protect yourself and your family from the invisible enemy. The principles are simple and can be learned by any school-age child. Furthermore, the techniques are 100% effective and can be researched in any public library.

The Whole Armor (Panoply) of God

Today's vocabulary word is *panoply*. It is a Greek word meaning the complete set of armor, shields and weapons that a soldier would take into battle.

Followers of Jesus are permitted to wear an invisible *panoply*. It is completely effective against the attacks of the enemy. But very few people actually bother wearing it. There are two reasons:

- **Eligibility.** Not everybody who calls himself or herself a Christian is actually following Jesus. Most folks are drifting through a comfortable rut that might or might not include attending church.

- **Ignorance.** Many eligible Christians think spiritual warfare is for pastors or other folks. Most don't realize the danger they're in, or the protection they forfeit.

The apostle Paul vividly describes the need for the *panoply* in Ephesians 6, verses 11–13:

¹¹ Put on the whole armor (*panoply*) of God so that you may be able to stand against the wiles of the devil. ¹² For we do not wrestle against flesh and blood, but against principalities, against powers, against the world's rulers, of the darkness of this age, against spiritual wickedness in high places. ¹³ Therefore take to yourselves the whole armor (*panoply*) of God, that you may be able to withstand in the evil day, and having done all, to stand. (*NKJV*)

Verse 11 makes it clear that the devil and his henchmen actively plot and set traps for people. When these plots come to light, as in the aftermath of September 11, we realize that nobody is able to completely escape "the wiles" of the enemy. Without special preparation, we won't be able to stand against them.

Verse 12 gives us a brief glimpse into the devil's chain of command. There are greater and lesser demon spirits assigned to geographic regions and to specific projects. Since our enemy is spiritual and attacks us with invisible weapons, we need spiritual armor and weapons not available in earthly gun shops.

With our normal eyesight, we can't see these monsters directly. But we can read history books and see how demon-possessed men and women have cut a bloody swath through people of every generation. Many of you reading this book are old enough to remember Adolph Hitler, one of the more-recent and more-remarkable puppets of the devil. Hitler was typical of these evil leaders, who usually reserve their worst attacks for Jewish and Christian people.

Verse 13 is an exhortation to every believer. The armor is freely available to you. It is guaranteed to be 100% effective in helping you withstand the enemy. It might save your life of somebody in your family.

The next five verses (14–18) describe the *panoply* in some detail:

¹⁴ Therefore stand, having your loins girded about with truth, and having on the breastplate of righteousness ¹⁵ and your feet shod with the preparation of the gospel of peace. ¹⁶ Above all, take the shield of faith, with which you shall be able to quench all the fiery darts of the wicked. ¹⁷ And take the helmet of salvation, and the sword of the Spirit, which is the Word of God, ¹⁸ praying always with all prayer and supplication in *the* Spirit. (*MKJV*)

Let's look at the *panoply*, item by item.

"Loins girt about with truth . . ."

In biblical times, men wore long robes. As a first step in preparing for battle or to run, the men would bind the lower part of the robe around their waist. Picture a man reaching down through his ankles, grabbing the back hem of the robe, and pulling it forward and upward to tuck into his belt. This would make a large "diaper," freeing his legs to run and providing a little protective padding to his groin area.

Having your "loins girt about with truth" means making a commitment to the truth, to avoid becoming entangled in the lies of the enemy. Truth must be more important to you than your personal agenda, your family, your job, your religious rut or even your life itself. You must learn the truth and be committed, in advance, to acting upon it.

Remember that Jesus said, "I am the Way, the Truth, and the Light." As part of your study, you must examine the claims of Jesus to see if He really is the Truth. If His claims are true, then He must be the Way. If He is the Way, we must follow Him on His terms.

Jesus described the connection between light and truth in the Gospel of John, chapter 3, verses 19–21:

> [19] And this is the condemnation, that the Light has come into the world, and men loved darkness rather than the Light, because their deeds were evil. [20] For everyone who does evil hates the Light, and does not come to the Light, lest his deeds should be exposed. [21] But he who practices truth comes to the Light so that his works may be revealed, that they exist, having been worked in God. (MKJV)

Your commitment to the truth includes being transparent and consistent. Your integrity will require you to come to the light. As a minimum, you will need to confront your own shortcomings and failings. At times, you will need to confess your faults to your spouse or to your pastor when you have fallen short.

In the 8th chapter of John's gospel, Jesus described another benefit of a lifetime commitment to truth and integrity:

> [31] Then Jesus said to the Jews who believed on Him, "If you continue in My Word, you are My disciples indeed. [32] "And you shall know the truth, and the truth shall make you free." (MKJV)

Your integrity and transparency will set you free from bondage to things of this world. Without a commitment to truth, your life will grow increasingly dark and you will become a slave to the entrapments of the enemy.

Paul also warned about the connection between truth and light in the first chapter of his letter to the Romans:

> [18] For the wrath of God is revealed from Heaven against all ungodliness and unrighteousness of men, who suppress the truth in unrighteousness, [19] because the thing which may be known of God is clearly revealed within them, for God revealed it to them. [20] For the unseen things of Him from the creation of the world are clearly seen, being realized by the things that are made, even His eternal power and Godhead, for them to be without excuse. [21] Because, knowing God, they did not glorify Him as God, neither were thankful. But they became vain in their imaginations, and their foolish heart was darkened. (MKJV)

The truth of God is readily available to any honest seeker. Next time you walk outside, look around at the grass and trees and birds. Somebody designed all those living things. Look at your own body. Somebody really smart designed your eyes and ears and senses. Somebody really smart designed your heart and lungs and muscles. Can you design an insect? Can you design an insect that can fly? Can you design an insect that can fly and produce honey and build wax honeycomb structures? Me neither.

According to verse 18 above, my college professors (and yours?) were not just ignorant of the truth. They were unwilling to live in accordance to the truth, so they actively suppressed or distorted the truth. As a result, according to verse 21, their foolish hearts were darkened.

Your first item of armor, then, is to commit your heart to discover and respond to the truth. Truth and light travel together, and your enemy cannot stand to be near either for fear of exposure.

"Having on the breastplate of righteousness"

Once you have prepared your heart by committing to follow the Truth, you must protect your heart from attack. Put simply, you must take care to avoid being led astray by your own emotions or cravings.

The word picture of a breastplate is very appropriate. A physical breastplate protects your vital organs from attack. Unlike a shield that must be held and manipulated with conscious effort, the breastplate is positioned during your daily preparation for battle. For the rest of the day, the breastplate protects your heart from clubs and arrows no matter what your hands are busy doing.

The spiritual breastplate of righteousness works in a similar way. It does not attach itself to us by accident. It's built up from the daily decisions we make about the key priorities of our lives. In Matthew 6, verses 19–21, Jesus commands us to set our hearts on eternal treasures:

> [19] Do not lay up treasures on earth for yourselves, where moth and rust corrupt, and where thieves break through and steal. [20] But lay up treasures in Heaven for yourselves, where neither moth nor rust corrupt, and where thieves do not break through nor steal. [21] For where your treasure is, there will your heart be also. *(MKJV)*

The issues involved are actually pretty simple, according to Jesus. God only gives us two primary commandments, and both involve our priorities and affections. Jesus gave these two commandments in Matthew 22, verses 37–40:

> [37] Jesus said to him, "You shall love the Lord your God with all your heart, and with all your soul, and with all your mind. [38] "This is the first and great commandment. [39] "And the second *is* like it, You shall love your neighbor as yourself. [40] "On these two commandments hang all the Law and the Prophets." *(MKJV)*

Jesus' commands are simple, but not easy. In fact, they're really backwards, like all the other great truths of the Bible. How can we possibly love an invisible God, Who cannot be detected with our natural senses? Worse yet, how can we love others like ourselves when our natural senses assure us that are neighbors are as weak and unlovable as we are?

Consider the implications. In your natural strength, you cannot comply with either of Jesus' two commandments. Compliance requires a miracle.

Following Jesus requires a God-centered life. Such a life is only possible after God miraculously changes your heart, in response to your faith. And you can only protect your heart from sneak attack by daily renewing your commitment to the righteous walk of faith.

The breastplate of righteousness, therefore, is a commitment to love God and to walk with Him in faith, in accordance with His Scriptures.

This is not a simple once-in-a-lifetime decision. It is a daily discipline of studying the Bible, praying for wisdom, and living in accordance with the Truth.

Don't underestimate the strength of the attacks, which are usually subtle and deceptive. Our common enemy will try to feed your natural affections and passions, to lure you away from God and your family. A small distraction can become a fatal attraction, if your heart is not protected. The attack can even be disguised as something helpful or good for you.

God knows your needs. At times, He will use supernatural means to satisfy your needs if you trust Him to keep His promises. By contrast, the enemy tempts us to take shortcuts for things we "need." He comes to us whispering:

- "You're a single person; you *need* some physical companionship . . ."
- "It's been a rough week; you *need* a few drinks . . ."
- "You're short on cash this month; you *need* to pad your expense report a little . . ."
- "You haven't eaten in two days; you *need* to steal that pastry . . ."
- "You can't *afford* to pay taxes on all the jobs where you were paid in cash. You *need* to cheat on your income tax . . ."

All of us pass through "wilderness" experiences, where we must walk in faith despite circumstances that appear to defy God's promises. Each day, we must renew our heart commitment to love God and trust Him to keep His word.

Special note to men: For us, the breastplate of righteousness includes a pair of optical filters, to keep us from being led astray by attractive women around us. Part of our daily armament is a commitment to not take a second look (or an extended first look) at a woman who is not our spouse. We must study and pray over our spouses' needs, not their faults.

Special note to women: For you, the breastplate of righteousness includes sound filters, to keep you from hearing or saying hurtful things. You must daily resist the temptation to use your God-given verbal skills for harm. Listen to and speak with God, not the TV or telephone.

"Feet shod with the preparation of the gospel of peace"

The third part of the armor is preparation for a long journey. You must prepare to follow Jesus wherever he leads.

Following Jesus will take you to places that require change and personal growth. You have probably already experienced some of those changes, and more changes await you tomorrow.

Long journeys require preparation. Following Jesus will bring you to places that you never expected. You will need to stock up on the spiritual equivalent of provisions and maps in order to navigate the road ahead.

The enemy will try to throw briars and boulders into your path. Without the right covering, your feet won't last the trip. Make the decision, in faith and in advance, that you will follow Jesus nonstop from here to the next life. Trust in God's power and protection to get you through, and He will not disappoint you.

"The shield of faith . . ."

Let's review Ephesians 6 verse 16:

[16] Above all, take the shield of faith, with which you shall be able to quench all the fiery darts of the wicked. (*MKJV*)

At the direction of the Holy Spirit, Paul introduces our shield with the words, "Above all . . ." This tells us that faith is the most-important part of our armor.

Our English word *shield* translates the Greek word *thureos*, a large door-shaped shield. It was large and sturdy enough to serve as a portable fortress. The soldier could prop it up and have both hands free to use a bow, sword or sling.

The Christian's shield is faith. It takes a certain type of faith to become a follower of Jesus. But the follower needs to develop more than bare-minimum faith, if he or she wants to survive the enemy's attacks.

Paul gives us a simple formula for building faith in Romans 10:
[17] So then faith cometh by hearing, and hearing by the word of God.

You cannot have faith in a vacuum of ignorance. You get faith by hearing and acting upon the truth, which is found in Scripture. The more quality time you spend studying and praying over the Scriptures, the more you abide in the truth of Jesus Christ.

In the verse above, *word* translates the Greek noun *rhema*. This is not the same as *logos*, which is ordinarily used to describe Scripture. The word *logos*, in a biblical context, refers to all that can be known about God, embodied in Jesus and recorded in Scripture. By contrast, *rhema* implies something spoken, especially at the direction of the Holy Spirit.

To illustrate the difference, picture yourself prayerfully studying the Scripture (the *logas*) as a daily discipline. At times, the Holy Spirit will make certain passages alive to your heart. For confirmation, He may also speak to you through the words of your pastor or another brother or sister whom you trust.

Faith is conviction, expressed in action, performed in obedience on the truth of Scripture that has been confirmed to your heart. It builds your faith to listen to anointed men of God preaching and teaching the Bible. The specific spoken word gives life to the general written word.

When you are strong in your faith, the fiery arrows of the enemy won't destroy you. You will know the truth and act upon it. With the help of the Holy Spirit, you will also discern the lies, accusations and distortions of the enemy. The flaming arrows will bounce harmlessly off your shield.

But if the devil's flaming arrows land in a pile of doubt or confusion, you're in trouble. A British friend of mine, a recent convert, was lured into what he thought was a Christian Bible study. Instead, it was a meeting of the local Watchtower Society. Taking advantage of his ignorance of Scripture, the group "taught" him their warped view of God and the Bible. Fortunately, I was able to sense a different flavor to his e-mails and send him a detailed explanation of what this cult group really believed compared to the Bible, and where to find more information. Within days, my friend had done the research, discovered the distorted nature of their teachings, and confronted their leader with questions that exposed their deception.

My British friend had been set on fire by the darts of the enemy. But when the word (*rhema*) of God was spoken to him, he responded in faith. By faith, he was able to quench the flaming arrows and be strengthened in his walk with the Lord. And he was empowered to fight back using the sword of the Spirit, which we shall soon discuss.

"The Helmet of Salvation"

The Apostle John gives a simple reason for his first epistle, in chapter 5:

⁴ These things have I written unto you that believe on the name of the Son of God; that ye may know that ye have eternal life, and that ye may believe on the name of the Son of God.

The first key phrase is: ". . . that ye may know that ye have eternal life . . ." This is an important truth. The follower of Jesus doesn't need to wait until Judgment Day to see if he'll somehow sneak into Heaven. The follower of Jesus can be sure of his salvation right now.

The second key phrase is: ". . . believe on the name of the Son of God." We intuitively know that we can't be perfect enough to deserve Heaven. However, any of you reading this book can have saving faith in the completed sacrifice of Jesus on the cross. We have peace with God, and we can have peace with our own turbulent thoughts.

The helmet of salvation, then, is having full assurance that our salvation depends on the merits of Jesus rather than the merits of our own good works. This helmet protects your thought processes, to keep you from being ensnared or distracted by religious tradition and false doctrines.

Some denominations never present the clear, Scriptural teaching of salvation by faith, as explained in the earlier chapters of this book. Instead, many have devised complicated systems of beliefs and practices built up over the centuries and enshrined in tradition. People can be devout members of these churches, fulfilling as many regulations as they can grasp, but they can never be assured of their salvation since (in the eyes of the religious leaders) their salvation is tied to their works.

If you aren't really sure about your salvation, your mind is vulnerable to attack from all sides. Take a few minutes to backtrack and reread the first few chapters of this book. There's a shiny, new helmet waiting there for you, and it's just your size.

If your denomination has lots of traditional beliefs, please study the Scripture yourself to gain assurance of salvation. Don't let the religious folks and traditions deprive you of your helmet. You'll need it in battle.

"The sword of the Spirit, which is the Word of God"

The Greek word for sword in this passage is *machaira*. It refers to a personal weapon, like a dirk or dagger or knife. This sword is a powerful weapon for good, when you learn to use it.

A few paragraphs earlier, we looked at the difference between the *logos* of God and the *rhema* of God. The *logos* is the Scripture, the truth about God, embodied in Jesus and written down in our Bibles. The *logos* is God's plan for your life, His general revealed word. On the other hand, the Bible also speaks of the *rhema* of God—a portion of the *logos* that is spoken by the Holy Spirit to the heart of a believer. The *rhema* is the Holy Spirit's word to your heart for your situation.

When God Himself speaks His word (*rhema*) to you, it is usually by quickening a Scripture to your heart—one that you have already studied. When you take action based on His *rhema*, you are acting in faith. You can move forward in full confidence that God will keep all His specific promises to you.

When (not if) the enemy attacks you, ask God for a *rhema*—a Scripture that the Holy Spirit will bring to your attention and energize on your behalf. A perfect example is in Matthew 4, verses 1–3, when Jesus demonstrated the sword of the Spirit:

> [1] Then Jesus was led by the Spirit up into the wilderness, to be tempted by the devil. [2] And when He had fasted forty days and forty nights, He was afterwards hungry. [3] And when the tempter came to Him, he said, "If You are *the* Son of God, command that these stones be made bread." (MKJV)

During an extended fast, the body stops feeling hungry after about a week. When hunger returns—typically at the 40-day point—the body is beginning to die.

In verse 2 we see that Jesus' hunger had returned. His physical body was warning Him of impending death. So the devil tempted Jesus to use His supernatural power to gratify His own physical cravings. It would be a "victim-less crime." Some folks would even call it a good idea. Certainly there was nothing immoral about the bread itself.

But Jesus did not turn the rocks into bread, because He saw the larger picture. His Father had given Him power for ministry purposes, so the power was holy—dedicated completely to accomplishing God's plan. Furthermore, His Father had given Him other promises concerning physical needs. Jesus was dying, but He still had choices, as we see in verse 4:

> [4] But He answered and said, "It is written, 'Man shall not live by bread alone, but by every word that proceeds out of the mouth of God.'" (MKJV)

In verse 4, Jesus used *rhema* to describe the word of God that keeps man alive. And Jesus used the *rhema* of God as a *machaira* to fight back the attack of Satan.

The point is that we must study God's word—the Bible or *logos*—to fill our hearts with weapons that God can energize at the appropriate time. Then, when His Holy Spirit speaks the *rhema* to our hearts, we must act in complete obedience.

There's another peculiar aspect to this passage that isn't obvious from the English translation. The *rhema* is the sword of the Spirit. It is His weapon. His hand holds the Sword, and His power makes it effective.

The Holy Spirit Himself is using the sword, and not always against the enemy. Sometimes He uses it as a scalpel, deftly trimming away something in my life, or cutting away the blinders that have kept me from understanding His will. I've learned not to grab for the sword, because the sharp end might be pointed at my own heart. I trust the Holy Spirit to use this weapon on my behalf.

". . . Praying always . . . in the Spirit . . ."

For this critical part of our armor, Paul drops the word pictures, as we see in verse 18:

> [18] Praying always with all prayer and supplication in the Spirit, and watching thereunto with all perseverance and supplication for all saints.

Instead of a colorful metaphor (e.g. helmet, shield), Paul gives the technical specifications for the type of prayer that can save your neck in battle.

Let's take the specifications word by word:

- **Praying**: On a personal level, prayer is communicating with God, sharing our hearts and listening for His. On a different level, prayer is the battlefield communications system that enables the Commander in Chief to stay connected with you, to keep you tuned into His will and His heart. Only the discipline of prayer can activate your *panoply* (armor) and empower you to use it effectively.

- **Always**: Translates three words in the Greek meaning at every opportunity. Your daily stewardship (your job or ministry) requires diligent attention, but there will still be pauses and transition times when you can rejoice and praise God for His faithfulness. There will also be times of outright attack, especially if you're tired or weak. If you begin the day with intense, strategic prayers, you can get through the day with short, tactical prayers. If you begin the day without prayer, your battlefield prayers will be less effective and you're susceptible to attack.

- **All prayer**: God appreciates every type of sincere prayer, especially the worshipful prayer of praise and adoration. It is always appropriate to praise God for His love, His character and His faithfulness. Be sure to praise God with your physical voice as often as possible, because it will reverberate through your entire body and give you strength.

- **All supplication**: Supplication is asking specific favors of God. Study the examples of effective prayer in the Bible. They usually were requests for God to keep His promises that appeared to be contradicted by the circumstances. We must pray for God to energize His Scriptural promises, that His Name and His Word may be honored.

- **In the Spirit**: Our prayer is to be directed by the Holy Spirit, as we let Him pray through us in tongues (see earlier chapter) and with our understanding. In this way, we allow the Holy Spirit to direct our prayers, for God's will to be done and His power to prevail. If God Himself prays through you to accomplish His will, you can't lose.

- **And watching**: God calls us to be awake, sleepless, vigilant. God's love gives us peace and casts out fear. But "peaceful" is not the same as "comfortable." If we get too comfortable, we're vulnerable to ambush.

- **All perseverance**: Prayer takes time and persistence. God's will has a desired outcome, and our hearts burn to achieve that outcome. But His will also has a desired schedule, and we seldom want to hear about it. We must want God's will badly enough to weep for it, and sincerely enough to wait for it.

- **Supplication for all saints**: Your brothers and sisters have needs. Some of God's promises are not coming true in their lives. The Holy Spirit wants permission to pray His promises into existence through you, for their benefit.

Just remember that there are different types of prayer to accomplish different purposes. Praying in tongues all day at work is helpful, as part of your daily armor. It is not a substitute for getting alone with God early in the morning and late at night. Your short daytime prayers will only be as effective as your long morning prayers.

Think about your Bible-and-prayer time this morning. Was *that* prayer effective enough to stop a raging demon in his tracks? Would your bedtime prayers last night have been effective in raising your uncle from his sickbed of cancer?

Put it on

Your armor is wonderful and completely effective. But are you making best use of it? Do you wear it often enough to be confident in it? Are you praying enough to stay in two-way communication with the Commander in Chief? Strive to wear your *panoply* every day, so that you may sing like King David in Psalm 18:

> [30] *As for God, His way is* perfect; the Word of Jehovah *is* tried; He *is a* shield to all those who trust in Him. [31] For who *is* God besides Jehovah? Or, who *is* a Rock except our God? [32] *It is* God who girds me with strength and makes my way perfect. [33] He makes my feet like hinds' feet, and sets me on my high places. [34] He teaches my hands to war, so that a bow of bronze is bent by my arms. [35] You have also given me the shield of Your salvation; and Your right hand has held me up, and Your gentleness has made me great. [36] You have given a wide place for my steps under me, so that my feet have not slipped. [37] I have pursued my enemies and overtaken them; nor did I turn again until they were destroyed. [38] I have shattered them, and they cannot rise again; they have fallen under my feet. [39] For You have girded me with strength for the battle; You have humbled under me those who rose up against me. (MKJV)

Closing Prayer: Lord, forgive me for not taking full advantage of this wonderful panoply. I repent of not praying enough to use it effectively. Thank you for this armor and for the victory you will give me this day. Amen.

Durable Joy

Chapter 10

B-Team

God's Peculiar People

And the LORD hath chosen thee to be a peculiar people unto himself, above all the nations that are upon the earth. *Deuteronomy 14:2*

Opening Prayer: Lord, I'm sure of my faith in You, but some of my brothers and sisters in the Church really look funny to me. Please open my heart to Your plan, and give me discernment of how this all fits together to your glory, I pray.

*O*ne of the rudest shocks of the Christian life is discovering that you're surrounded by what God calls "peculiar people." Worse yet, they're just like you.

These people are your teammates. Welcome to the B-Team.

Years ago, Dr. J. Vernon McGee said that new believers find two things especially hard to accept: God's program, and God's people. He was right on target. God's program is so peculiar that much of it looks backwards to us. And we believers are a pretty odd-looking bunch. The strangest part is that the two concepts are interrelated.

The Apostle Paul was quite blunt about this in First Corinthians 1, verses 25–29:

[25] Because the foolishness of God is wiser than men; and the weakness of God is stronger than men. [26] For behold your calling, brethren, that not many wise after the flesh, not many mighty, not many noble, are called. [27] But God chose the foolish things of the world, that He might put to shame them that are wise; and God chose the weak things of the world, that He might put to shame the things that are strong; [28] and the base things of the world, and the things that are despised, did God choose, *yea* and the things that are not, that He might bring to nought the things that are: [29] that no flesh should glory before God.

Did you grasp that? God chose you *because* you were weak or foolish or both. That way, everybody will know that any good work coming from you can only be because of God's life-changing power.

God knows that our human nature is prideful and selfish. He wants to do mighty works through us, but He will not share His glory with anybody else. So He chooses notorious fools and weaklings like me to teach other fools like you. We're quite a match, don't you think?

This is backwards from the way we chose up teams for sandlot baseball or flag football when we were kids. The captains of the two teams would take turns selecting the biggest, strongest available players. For a one-hour game, no player was chosen for his long-term developmental potential.

God has a better idea, because He has an eternal perspective. His plan is to give us a supernatural heart transplant, and a new nature that can live forever in the presence of our holy, almighty God. He does this to shame the prideful folks who are so content with their fleshly looks and abilities right now.

We see this principle expressed in the Old Testament in Psalm 8, verse 2:

[2] Out of the mouth of babes and nursing infants You have ordained strength, because of Your enemies, that You may silence the enemy and the avenger. (NKJV)

Have you seen a newborn baby lately? My first grandchild was a few days old when I first held her. At that time, she had not yet acquired any strength or agility. She relied on her parents and grandparents for everything.

God wants us to approach Him the same way, weak and dependent upon Him. He wants us to trust Him to provide strength, guidance and protection. That way, when we find joy in times of trouble, or operate powerfully in the gifts of the Holy Spirit, the power is conspicuously from Him and not of ourselves.

Gifts in Perspective: God's Plan

As we said in an earlier chapter, God gives us the gifts of the Holy Spirit to build up His Church, the body of Jesus Christ. The gifts may seem odd from a human standpoint, but God has a Plan. In 1 Corinthians 12, verses 11–14 we read His Plan:

> [11] But one and the same Spirit works all these things, distributing to each one individually as He wills. [12] For as the body is one and has many members, but all the members of that one body, being many, are one body, so also is Christ. [13] For by one Spirit we were all baptized into one body—whether Jews or Greeks, whether slaves or free—and have all been made to drink into one Spirit. [14] For in fact the body is not one member but many. *(NKJV)*

You're probably smarter than me, so maybe you understand these verses perfectly. But the more I study them, the crazier they look.

Yes, I understand that the gifts are personally distributed by the Holy Spirit. I can even understand that He gives us gifts individually, according to His own plan. But how can these individual gifts—operating through rebellious, self-centered vessels like us—possibly make us into something resembling a unified body? How can this body, consisting of such flawed individuals, ever live up to the title of the "body of Christ?"

Please don't take this lightly. I'm a life-long student of human nature and group behavior. I've read hundreds of books, looking for answers about why people act the way they do. The more I learn about human nature, the less I trust it.

Isn't human nature grand and noble?

Not so you'd notice. We're selfish. We're weak. We cave in to temptation. We quit under pressure. We quit even before the pressure begins. We're always looking for the easy way, the convenient way. We intuitively resist the activities that will strengthen us. We eat the foods that destroy our health. We'll willingly risk a lifetime of suffering and side effects in hopes of enjoying a few moments of illicit worldly pleasure.

Would you trust the eternal future of the human race—to humans?

God did—but He didn't trust our future to human nature. He entrusts our future in the operation of His Holy Spirit through the agency of human believers.

Amazingly, His plan works. At times, some of us get it right. At times, enough of us in a particular group submit our rebellious hearts to the leading of the Holy Spirit. At times, collectively, we resemble the body of Christ. At times, unbelievers come into our assemblies and sense the presence of the Lord and surrender their hearts to Jesus. At times, we minister to each other. At times, the Holy Spirit works healings and prophecies and words of wisdom through these mortal bodies of ours. It's a miracle.

Gift Ministries: The Body In Action

So how does all this work? We've read lots of Scripture about the gifts of the Holy Spirit. And we've read lots about how each of us function as parts of the body of Christ. But how does all this look in real life? How do the gifts work to knit us together as a functioning entity?

Verses 27–28 give us insight into this mystery:

> [27] Now you are the body of Christ, and members individually. [28] And God has appointed these in the church: first apostles, second prophets, third teachers, after that miracles, then gifts of healings, helps, administrations, varieties of tongues. *(NKJV)*

In the first part of this chapter, Paul described gifts that the Holy Spirit gives to individuals. Now these verses explain that God gives us *individuals with these gifts* to minister within the church. Let's discuss these briefly.

Apostles

The term "apostles" is usually reserved for the disciples personally chosen by our Lord during His earthly ministry (the original 12, less Judas) plus Paul/Saul of Tarsus. In Scripture, we have no record of disciples being ordained as apostles.

The Greek word *apostellos,* translated "apostle," means "one sent forth." It implies a sender, a message and a specific mission to accomplish.

In addition to the 12 men mentioned above, other individuals are described as apostles:

- In Acts 14:14, Paul and Barnabus are described as apostles.

- In Romans 16:7, two men—Andronicus and Junia—are described as "outstanding among the apostles . . ."

- In Galatians 1:19, Paul says he ". . . saw none of the apostles except James, the Lord's brother."

- In Hebrews 3:1, Jesus is described as "the Apostle and High Priest of our confession." In this context, Jesus was the first Apostle: He was sent forth by the Father to personally bring the precious message of redemption to fallen mankind.

In my personal opinion, the Lord still anoints and sends apostles to the church today. We certainly still have need of them. These men do the same tasks that the original 11 Apostles did immediately after Pentecost. They preach, they teach, they plant churches. They disciple others to carry the Gospel message and plant other churches.

Apostles are more than just successful pastors and teachers. They are more than just evangelists. They carry the seeds of planting entire church bodies. They demonstrate a hundred-fold or a thousand-fold fruitfulness in training other men and women to reach their full ministry potential.

Apostles may operate in all the gifts of the Spirit. As one pastor described it: "I look inside myself and don't see any gifts. But the Holy Spirit lives inside me, and He has all the gifts."

Prophets

God gives prophets to the Church to serve as evangelists, pastors and counselors. In ministry context, we say these individuals function in the office of the prophet. They speak forth God's Word with clarity and consistency, to edify the individual members of the body of Christ.

Of course, men and women may operate in the gift of prophecy outside the formal context of ordained ministry, as we discussed earlier. In all cases, the Holy Spirit speaks through submitted vessels to build up all the members of the body.

Teachers

The third gift ministry is teaching. Teachers make Scriptures come alive in the minds and hearts of individual believers. Teachers are not evangelists, nor do they generally function as prophets to the assembled congregation.

Some evangelists, pastors and prophets are also gifted as teachers. However, their ministry is to the congregation at large. Teachers are entrusted with the responsibility of working with believers individually and in small groups. A few teachers, like Chuck Missler, have become so popular that large groups gather whenever they speak. Nevertheless, all true teachers live for the opportunity of making God's Word real for people, and delight to share with individuals and small groups where they can directly interact with their students.

". . . after that miracles, then gifts of healings, helps, administrations, varieties of tongues."

Apostles, prophets and teachers are the three most-visible gift ministries. Then come these five: miracles, healings, helps, administrations and tongues. Like the first three, their operation is essential to the healthy functioning of the body.

- **Miracles** and **healings**, as discussed earlier, are a direct result of a believer's personal prayer life. If we are really praying in the Spirit, we are in two-way communication with God. If we actively listen to God, He will reveal His will for miracles and healings. If we act in faith according to His will, God will perform miracles and healings.

- Helps and administrations are very dear to the heart of God, because they involve giving. **Helps** is easy to understand. A Spirit-filled believer is always ready to sacrificially help another person. The gift of **administrations** is something quite different and special. It involves planning, organizing and carrying out church programs. Some is done by pastors and church administrators. Some is done by volunteers. Unlike worldly administration, God's work cannot be done with fleshly talents. God's administration is always an act of faith, performed at the direction of the Holy Spirit.

- The gift of **tongues** is valuable for building up individual believers and sometimes helpful in group settings. In prayer meetings that are primarily "believers-only" gatherings, praying in tongues can be helpful. In such cases, the Holy Spirit can speak praise and worship through us, to help tune our hearts to His goals for the group. As we'll see in another chapter, our prayer language is not a suitable vehicle for delivering prophetic messages to a group.

Let's read verses 29 and 30:

[29] Are all apostles? Are all prophets? Are all teachers? Are all workers of miracles? [30] Do all have gifts of healings? Do all speak with tongues? Do all interpret? *(NKJV)*

The answer to these questions is self-evident. God gives gifts to whomever He pleases, for whatever reasons make sense to Him.

Pray earnestly to the Father to give you wisdom and courage regarding the gifts He gives you through His Holy Spirit. God wants you to be a healthy, contributing member of the church, the Body of Christ.

A Problem: Cancerous Christians

One of the church's biggest problem isn't the nonbelievers or attacks from outside. The biggest hindrance to church health is cancer within the body.

Chemically, there is very little difference between a cancer cell and a normal, healthy cell in your body. The primary difference is behavioral. The normal cell contributes to (and will sacrifice itself for) the survival of the body. The cancer cell is purely self-centered. The cancer cell will destroy other body parts in order to grow itself.

Likewise, a Cancerous Christian looks very much like any other. He or she may be a benign tumor, just taking up space. He or she may also be very active, attending services, singing songs, attending potlucks, reading books. Some Cancerous Christians actively seek, receive and visibly practice the gifts of the Holy Spirit. The Cancerous Christian often attends seminary and enters the ministry as a "career."

But the Cancerous Christian is primarily concerned with his or her personal "growth." The Cancerous Christian wants a platform to exercise his/her gifts. Cancerous Christians are ambitious, and often seek leadership positions and public recognition for their works. They start TV ministries. They collect money. They even create "prosperity gospel" messages to justify their lavish lifestyles.

These people are visible cancers, disfiguring the body of Christ. These are the hypocrites that our unsaved friends despise.

Cancerous Christians don't look or act much like Jesus.

The Cure for Cancer: Abiding in Jesus

God calls us to serve like Jesus. God calls us to arise up early, before sunrise, to seek His face and learn how we can serve Him each day. God calls us to repent of our selfish, self-centered, cancerous behavior.

God calls us to become servants, making the love of Jesus real for every person we meet. Every person is important in God's eyes. But we must become especially conscious of the needs of our brothers and sisters in Christ. Their spiritual health is important to us, even if the connection isn't obvious.

Why? Verses 15–19 give insight:

[15] If the foot should say, "Because I am not a hand, I am not of the body," is it therefore not of the body? [16] And if the ear should say, "Because I am not an eye, I am not of the body," is it therefore not of the body? [17] If the whole body were an eye, where would be the hearing? If the whole were hearing, where would be the smelling? [18] But now God has set the members, each one of them, in the body just as He pleased. [19] And if they were all one member, where would the body be? *(NKJV)*

The Church, the body of Christ, has a lot of diversity. In fact, there's often more diversity than we're comfortable with.

Admit it: you and I are really invested in being just exactly who we are. So if we've dedicated a lifetime to being ears, the feet will probably look very odd to us.

Verses 20–26 echo our earlier discussion of healthy believers vs. Cancerous Christians:

[20] But now indeed there are many members, yet one body. [21] And the eye cannot say to the hand, "I have no need of you"; nor again the head to the feet, "I have no need of you." [22] No, much rather, those members of the body which seem to be weaker are necessary. [23] And those members of the body which we think to be less honorable, on these we bestow greater honor; and our unpresentable parts have greater modesty, [24] but our presentable parts have no need. But God composed the body, having given greater honor to that part which lacks it, [25] that there should be no schism in the body, but that the members should have the same care for one another. [26] And if one member suffers, all the members suffer with it; or if one member is honored, all the members rejoice with it. *(NKJV)*

Verses 23–24 are pretty subtle. Paul is talking about our internal organs and private parts. These "less honorable" or "unpresentable" parts are adorned with clothing (". . . on these we bestow greater honor . . .").

Remember: the body of Christ is very complex and very diverse. It is a supernatural, spiritual entity. We can't begin to understand how our Lord operates through all of us to carry out His program. Yet somehow He makes everything work.

Go to Church

Now you understand that you are part of this B-Team. Now you realize that "B" stands for "Body"—the body of Christ. You are an integral part of this body, and your personal health depends on your relationship with the other body parts.

You can't do this from a distance, by mail or TV. You must get as involved as you can, for your particular situation. If you can walk and drive, you *should* get yourself to a Bible-believing church at least once per week. To get the most from your relationship, you should also become involved in a home fellowship group, if your church offers them.

Our need for fellowship is another backwards truth. Our faith in Jesus gives us individual access to the throne room of God, but we can't attain God's best apart from our relationship to other believers.

The epistle to the Hebrews gives an elegantly simple summary of this backwards truth, in chapter 10 verses 19–25:

> [19] Therefore, brethren, since we have confidence to enter the sanctuary by the blood of Jesus, [20] by the new and living way which He opened for us through the curtain, that is, through His flesh, [21] and since we have a great priest over the house of God, [22] let us draw near with a true heart in full assurance of faith, with our hearts sprinkled clean from an evil conscience and our bodies washed with pure water. [23] Let us hold fast the confession of our hope without wavering, for He who promised is faithful; [24] and let us consider how to stir up one another to love and good works, [25] not neglecting to meet together, as is the habit of some, but encouraging one another, and all the more as you see the Day drawing near. (*MKJV*)

Brothers and sisters, "the Day" is certainly drawing near. We must be increasingly diligent to meet together in regular fellowship with each other.

My Own Way . . .

People frequently tell me they can worship God their own way, without going to weekly church services. They have had bad experiences in local churches. Many times, the devil has attacked them through wolves in sheep's clothing.

Others might have come to the Lord by watching a TV pastor or listening to a Christian radio program. These have no experience in local churches, except perhaps in the lifeless church their parents attended.

To both of these, Jesus has a simple call: "Follow Me." Keep your eyes on Jesus and follow Him. Today, Jesus walks this earth in a composite body, made up of body parts that are individually weak.

Earnestly look for a local church that is teaching the Bible and where people are seeking the Lord with all their hearts.

If all the local churches within an hour's driving range are weak, then you still must be faithful. Let the Lord lead you to one church, and let Him work change through you as He works changes in you.

Remember that the "through you" changes must be done through the authority structure of the local church body. Even if you are more gifted and dynamic than the church leaders, you must respect the fact that God Himself has put those leaders in place for a season and for a reason. You must be like the Roman Centurion in Matthew chapter 8 verse 9 who told Jesus:

> [9] "For I am a man under authority, with soldiers under me; and I say to one, 'Go,' and he goes, and to another, 'Come,' and he comes, and to my slave, 'Do this,' and he does it." *(MKJV)*

The Roman soldier perfectly understood the concept of authority. He exercised great authority towards others under him because he willingly submitted to the authority of others over him.

The pastor in a church has authority because he submits to the authority of God, through the leading of the Holy Spirit. You will have authority in that local congregation only to the extent that you submit to the authority of the pastors and leaders over you. God Himself put those leaders in those positions. Each pastor or leader must answer to God for his or her faithfulness in that role.

This is yet another backwards truth. Your Gifts of the Holy Spirit come directly from God. However your authority in a local church comes through that congregation's leadership, not directly from God.

You might have a direct vision or dream from God that He wants you to help that church experience revival. But you must seek the Lord's guidance for working within the church's authority structure, to build up the whole body of Christ. Otherwise you will become a troublesome cancer, and your "growth" will harm those around you.

God's Peculiar People

We began this chapter with a quote from Deuteronomy chapter 14, verse 2:

And the LORD hath chosen thee to be a peculiar people unto himself, above all the nations that are upon the earth.

So far, we have had good-natured fun with the phrase "peculiar people," as God's people are called in the quaint language of the King James Version. To the modern reader, *peculiar* means odd, eccentric or otherwise deviant from the norm. To a great extent, the backwards nature of the Christian walk does make us look odd and eccentric to people outside the church.

However, we must not ignore what God intended here. *Peculiar* translates the Hebrew word *segullah* meaning treasured or stored up in a secure place.

To put this in perspective, let's review some of the Scriptures that refer to God's peculiar people. The first occurrence is Exodus chapter 19:

⁴ Ye have seen what I did unto the Egyptians, and how I bare you on eagles' wings, and brought you unto Myself. ⁵ Now therefore, if ye will obey My voice indeed, and keep My covenant, then ye shall be a **peculiar treasure** unto Me above all people: for all the earth is Mine: ⁶ And ye shall be unto Me a kingdom of priests, and an holy nation.

The Lord rescued the people of Israel from Egypt in a dramatic fashion. Likewise He rescued you and me, and paid for our redemption with the life of His only Son, Jesus. This makes you a very important person in God's eyes.

Did you notice all the personal pronouns referring to God in these three verses? You can count eight occurrences of "I, Me, My, Myself and Mine." Take a hint. God takes a very personal interest in you.

God views you as a special treasure. He has prepared a place in heaven to be your permanent home, so you may live forever near Him. He loves you, and wants you to abide in Him (". . . obey My voice . . ."). Your transformed life is proof of His love and faithfulness toward those who follow Jesus.

In Deuteronomy chapter 26, we see that God expects us to study and keep His commandments as part of a two-way pledge:

> [16] This day the LORD thy God hath commanded thee to do these statutes and judgments: thou shalt therefore keep and do them with all thine heart, and with all thy soul. [17] Thou hast avouched the LORD this day to be thy God, and to walk in His ways, and to keep His statutes, and His commandments, and His judgments, and to hearken unto His voice: [18] And the LORD hath avouched thee this day to be **His peculiar people**, as He hath promised thee, and that thou shouldest keep all His commandments; [19] And to make thee high above all nations which He hath made, in praise, and in name, and in honour; and that thou mayest be an holy people unto the LORD thy God, as He hath spoken.

When we avouch (pledge) to the Lord to follow Jesus, God avouches (pledges) to us that He will be faithful to love and cherish us as His peculiar (treasured) people. If we follow Him faithfully, abiding in Him and holding nothing back, He will open His arms wide to us.

In the New Testament, "peculiar" translates a Greek phrase *laos peripoiesis* that literally means "for His own possession." We find this phrase in two places, the first being in Paul's letter to Titus, chapter 2:

> [11] For the grace of God that bringeth salvation hath appeared to all men, [12] Teaching us that, denying ungodliness and worldly lusts, we should live soberly, righteously, and godly, in this present world; [13] Looking for that blessed hope, and the glorious appearing of the great God and our Saviour Jesus Christ; [14] Who gave himself for us, that He might redeem us from all iniquity, and purify unto Himself **a peculiar people**, zealous of good works.

Notice the context. Paul is writing that God's people should live differently than folks whose lives have not been touched by Jesus. His Holy Spirit can change our hearts to desire what God desires. God can give us victory over the cravings that formerly ruled our lives. He can also give us victory over selfishness, as we shall see.

The second appearance of this phrase can be found in Peter's first letter, chapter 2, verses 4–9:

[4] For having been drawn to Him, a living Stone, indeed rejected by men, but elect, precious with God; [5] you also as living stones are built up a spiritual house, a holy priesthood, to offer up spiritual sacrifices acceptable to God through Jesus Christ. [6] Therefore also it is contained in the Scripture: "Behold, I lay in Zion a chief corner Stone, elect, precious, and he who believes on Him shall never be ashamed." [7] Therefore to you who believe is the honor. But to those who are disobedient, He is the Stone which the builders rejected; this One came to be the Head of the corner, [8] and a Stone-of-stumbling and a Rock-of-offense to those disobeying, who stumble at the Word, to which they also were appointed. [9] But you are a chosen generation, a royal priesthood, a holy nation, a people for possession, so that you might speak of the praises of Him who has called you out of darkness into His marvelous light. (MKJV)

God calls us to come out of our former darkness and come to Jesus, the Light of the world. He should be our Head. We should seek to please Him in all we do. Our lives should be transformed by His Holy Spirit.

As individuals we must abide in Jesus with all our heart and strength. Then, as fully functional members of His body, we will love each other and give ourselves sacrificially to build up each other.

As individuals, we sometimes look peculiar to our family and friends who don't know Jesus. Nevertheless, our Father in Heaven views us as His peculiar treasure, and loves us with a love beyond measure.

Your Neighbors

In Jesus' day, the religious leaders enjoyed arguing about the Law. They frequently debated which commandment of the Law was greatest. When one of the rabbis asked Jesus for His opinion, His answer caught everybody by surprise:

[37] Jesus said to him, "You shall love the Lord your God with all your heart, and with all your soul, and with all your mind. [38] This is the first and great commandment. [39] And the second *is* like it, You shall love your neighbor as yourself. [40] On these two commandments hang all the Law and the Prophets."

Did you know that the two commandments are intertwined? It's true. If you spend quality time abiding in Jesus, it will change your heart. Your changed heart will be able to see your neighbors as God sees them. Your changed heart will inevitably love the unlovely people, because God loves them.

Your human heart cannot do this. A reporter once spent the day following Mother Theresa through the streets, amazed at her compassion for the sick and dying. "I wouldn't do that for a million dollars!" said the reporter. Mother Theresa replied, "Neither would I."

You cannot consciously develop compassion for your neighbors. Love, as we saw in an earlier chapter, is a Fruit of the Holy Spirit. Only the Holy Spirit can produce selfless love in your heart. If you are abiding in Jesus, the Holy Spirit will develop His love in you without your conscious effort.

Do you love the Lord your God with all your heart? Are you abiding daily in His presence? Are you letting Him change you into His image? If so, then God's people will be a special treasured possession to you. If not, they will just look peculiar.

Closing Prayer: Lord, Your love and power are too amazing to understand. I don't understand why you chose to make me a part of Your body here on earth, but I'm grateful. Thank you for choosing me to be your peculiar treasure. Show me how to minister to my brothers and sisters in Christ, that You may be glorified in all we do. Amen.

Chapter 11

Tongues of Men and Angels

A Peculiar Gift

"Though I speak with the tongues of men and of angels, but have not love, I have become sounding brass or a clanging cymbal." *1 Corinthians 13:1*

Opening Prayer: Father, I want to experience all the gifts that Your Holy Spirit will give me. Help me to grow in the knowledge and experience of your gifts, that I may become the person You would have me be. Amen.

*T*his lesson is about adding joy and depth to your prayer life. You can experience a great deal in the Lord without the gift of tongues, but the experience of tongues is a blessing that I hope you receive.

We studied the gifts of the Holy Spirit in a previous chapter. In 1 Corinthians chapter 12, verses 11–14, we see why the gifts were given:

¹¹ But one and the same Spirit works all these things, distributing to each one individually as He wills. ¹² For as the body is one and has many members, but all the members of that one body, being many, are one body, so also is Christ. ¹³ For by one Spirit we were all baptized

into one body—whether Jews or Greeks, whether slaves or free—and have all been made to drink into one Spirit. [14] For in fact the body is not one member but many. (*NKJV*)

When we are baptized with the Holy Spirit, we are baptized into the body of Christ. We are immersed into a life very different from our previous experience. Instead of being enslaved to our (sometimes harmful) body passions, we willingly submit to the nourishing Head-ship of Jesus Christ.

With His new life in our hearts through the ministry of the Holy Spirit, He is our Head. We suddenly discover that we have a new role to play, as part of a much larger body. We might not be happy with our present roles, but all roles are important to the survival of the body. Unlike physical body parts which are very specialized, you and I might discover ourselves playing different roles on different days—as the Holy Spirit directs.

You might find yourself very gifted in one respect, but absolutely clueless in certain other gifts of the Holy Spirit. This is normal. The Holy Spirit gives the gifts as He wills, not as we desire.

"Do all speak with tongues?"

Should *everybody* speak in tongues as evidence of Holy Spirit baptism? Some denominations have teachings like that. When I was a new believer, that doctrine caused me a lot of personal grief and confusion (more on this subject later). Fortunately, that doctrine can easily be dismissed by reading verses 27–30:

> [27] Now you are the body of Christ, and members individually. [28] And God has appointed these in the church: first apostles, second prophets, third teachers, after that miracles, then gifts of healings, helps, administrations, varieties of tongues. [29] Are all apostles? Are all prophets? Are all teachers? Are all workers of miracles? [30] Do all have gifts of healings? Do all speak with tongues? Do all interpret? (*NKJV*)

Notice that Paul repeats the principle that gifts are distributed by God to build up the Church, the body of Christ. God gives specific gifts to specific persons.

Notice, too, the wording of verses 29–30: "Are all apostles? Are all prophets? Are all teachers? Are all workers of miracles? Do all have gifts of healings? Do all speak with tongues? Do all interpret?"

In both the English and the original Greek, the sentence structure demands a negative response. The reader is forced to say, "No, we all have different gifts and different roles in which to exercise these gifts." The Holy Spirit directed Paul to put this clear statement here for a reason—He knew false teachers would arise to confuse God's people.

The above-mentioned doctrine is problematic for another reason: the gift of tongues is the easiest to fake. In fact, I've seen TV ministers lead new believers into "baby-talk" exercises, getting them to make sounds that mimic tongues. This is outrageous and blasphemous. The Holy Spirit has power. When He chooses to speak through a yielded vessel, that person will not need to make baby talk.

A Tongues-Tied Teacher

Your teacher came to the Lord in a Baptist church that did not encourage operating in the gifts of the Spirit. So I visited a Mens' Meeting at a nearby charismatic church, and came forward to be baptized with the Holy Spirit. Some men prayed for me but I didn't feel anything special. Singing angels didn't appear in the rafters. Tongues of fire didn't descend upon our heads. And I didn't speak with other tongues. Bummer.

Weeks went by, still no tongues. In the meantime, the Holy Spirit was using me strongly as a teacher to handicapped adults and in the outreach evangelism class. It seemed like I was operating in some of the gifts, but not tongues. Oddly enough, I'd see other people come to the Lord and get prayed for, and they'd start chattering in tongues right away, before they even knew why they should.

"Well, maybe the first prayer didn't work," I thought. Made another visit to that church and asked another couple of brothers to pray for me to be baptized with the Holy Spirit. This time, the group leader got two sentences into the prayer and suddenly stopped.

He looked at me and said, "You've already received the baptism of the Holy Spirit." I was dumbstruck. The Lord had interrupted the man's prayer and given him a **Word of Knowledge**. Something in my heart told me that the Word was 100% true.

"Well, I was prayed for, but didn't feel anything different afterwards," I said.

The brother then said one of the most profound statements I'd ever heard: "You must walk in the Holy Spirit baptism like you walk in your salvation: by faith, and not by sight or feelings." That was a **Word of**

Wisdom, and it hit me like a thunderbolt. I can't remember what happened later, except that I still wasn't speaking in tongues. Still didn't *feel* Spirit-filled. So now what?

The Breakthrough

Throughout all this, my driving passion was to experience the Lord like Moses and David did. I wanted to know God as intimately as the Psalmist who wrote Psalm 16, verse 11:

> [11] You will show me the path of life; In Your presence is fullness of joy;
> At Your right hand are pleasures forevermore.

I just knew that the Psalmist was telling the truth, and that inexhaustible joy was waiting for "whosover wills." But that joy seemed out of reach. Maybe the gift of tongues would help me break through.

After months of studying and praying, the day came when I couldn't wait any longer. Closed the book, got down on the floor and started praying. Told the Lord that I wasn't moving from that spot until I knew I was baptized with the Holy Spirit and fully connected to Him. After about 20 minutes, the Holy Spirit came over me in a most-unexpected way. Besides feeling His presence and His love, I began weeping for joy.

Brokenness

Weeping is a normal part of life for most people, but not for me. Your teacher was born with a very level-headed temperament. Mom used to say that I was an old man at two years old. Didn't laugh or cry much; just went about my business. Weeping was very unusual, until that prayer session. Ever since, weeping (or at least that welling-up feeling) has been one of the key ways that the Holy Spirit communicates His will to me.

Later I discovered the term "brokenness" and realized how it applies to believers. There are lots of other applications of brokenness in our daily lives:

- We say a dog is house-broken when it obeys its masters' wishes concerning toilet training.
- We say a horse is saddle-broken when it will tolerate being saddled and ridden by its owner.

- We say shoes are broken-in when the owner can comfortably wear them all day.

- A believer is broken, by the Holy Spirit, when he reaches the end of his own strength and surrenders in tears to the will of God. The believer can then be used by God to accomplish His purposes.

Until that experience, I had been as doctrinally correct as a person could be. But I didn't experience the full depth of God's presence and power until I hit the limits of my strength.

Maybe your natural strength makes you feel smug and self-sufficient, but you shouldn't trust it. Your strength is worthless to God. He doesn't need your help. And He's willing to let you flounder and sink as long as *you* are in control of your own life. There is no combination of words (mis)quoted from Scripture that can force God to help you.

Psalm 34, verses 17–19, is a picture of what moves the Lord to help us:

> [17] The righteous cry out, and the Lord hears, and delivers them out of all their troubles. [18] **The Lord is near to those who have a broken heart, and saves such as have a contrite spirit.** [19] Many are the afflictions of the righteous, but the Lord delivers him out of them all. *(NKJV)*

If you're too comfortable to experience brokenness in prayer, then verse 19 above should make you think. Righteous people do experience afflictions, as we'll see in the chapters on "Brokenness" and "Blessings." The Lord will break us and re-shape us, if we permit Him. Likewise He will speak in tongues through us, if we permit Him.

Well, did you speak in tongues *then*?

No, and that was OK. The Lord spoke to me in the brokenness, and that was what I really wanted.

Years later, I asked the Lord, "Why not tongues?" The Lord replied that too many charismatic pastors experienced tongues before they reached brokenness, and that too many teachers associated tongues with deep prayer. The Lord told me He wanted me to clearly teach about deep prayer and intercession as separate activities from the experience of tongues.

Years later, in a home fellowship group, the tongues began for me as a tickle in the back of my throat. Later it developed into more of a prayer language as I prayed and practiced.

The point is that God wants us to pursue *Him* in prayer. That is our primary responsibility as believers. We are commanded to seek His face whether we speak in tongues or not.

Continuing with our passage in I Corinthians, Paul conveys a profound truth in chapter 13, verses 1–3:

> [1] Though I speak with the tongues of men and of angels, but have not **love**, I have become sounding brass or a clanging cymbal. [2] And though I have the gift of prophecy, and understand all mysteries and all knowledge, and though I have all faith, so that I could remove mountains, but have not **love**, I am nothing. [3] And though I bestow all my goods to feed the poor, and though I give my body to be burned, but have not **love**, it profits me nothing. (*NKJV*)

In our chapter on the Fruit of the Spirit, we saw that the Fruit of the Spirit is evidence of the Holy Spirit's life-changing work in our hearts. The fruit consists of character traits, of which love is foremost. If there is no love evident in your character, you'll have a difficult time convincing me that the Holy Spirit has been at work in your heart recently.

Let's see what these 3 verses tell us:

- The Holy Spirit gives gifts (prophecy, wisdom, faith, healings, miracles, tongues, etc.) to us, and produces fruit in our lives (love and other character traits).

- This same Holy Spirit, speaking through Paul, declares that the fruit—especially love—is more important than the gifts.

- Without love, my tongues mean nothing.

- Without love, I have nothing.

- Without love, I am nothing.

- Without love, all my benevolent works profit me nothing.

- Without love, being a martyr is a waste of time.

This passage echoes what Jesus Himself said in Matthew 7:

[22] "Many will say to Me in that day, 'Lord, Lord, have we not prophesied in Your name, cast out demons in Your name, and done many wonders in Your name?'

[23] "And then I will declare to them, 'I never knew you; depart from Me, you who practice lawlessness!'" (MKJV)

When the Holy Spirit is at work in your heart, love will be evident in your life. You will become more like Jesus, and He will know you intimately.

When people of different ages, genders and nationalities allow the Holy Spirit to work in their lives, they become more like Jesus and more like each other. Two people that selflessly love each other should find it easy to agree on important matters.

In the upcoming chapter on "Boldness," we will have more to say about the transforming power of God's love.

The Greatest of These

Paul summarizes Chapter 13 with this awesome thought:

[13] And now abide faith, hope, love, these three; but the greatest of these is love. *(MKVJ)*

This verse should trouble a thoughtful reader. How can love be greater than faith? After all, we're saved by faith. And hope (in our eternal future) is a natural result of saving faith in Jesus. How can love be greater than these?

Love is greater because love, as God defines it, can only arise from the Holy Spirit working in the heart of a believer. Faith in Jesus must surely come first. But love, the fruit of the Holy Spirit, is the inevitable proof that the believer is both trusting and abiding in Jesus. God expects us to bear this fruit. Enough said.

Moving on to 1 Corinthians 14, let's read the first 2 verses:

[1] Pursue love, and desire spiritual gifts, but especially that you may prophesy. [2] For he who speaks in a tongue does not speak to men but to God, for no one understands him; however, in the spirit he speaks mysteries. *(MKJV)*

Here are several important truths:

- Love is important, and we can cultivate that fruit of the Holy Spirit in our lives by abiding in Jesus.

- It is proper to desire spiritual gifts.

- Although the Holy Spirit selectively gives His gifts to believers, we are encouraged to ask for them. In fact, Paul writes this as a command. We are to actively seek the gifting of the Holy Spirit, to be empowered to serve and build up the body of Christ.

- Of all the gifts of the Holy Spirit, Paul (under the inspiration of the Holy Spirit) tells us that prophecy is the most helpful to the body of Christ.

With the notable exception of the Day of Pentecost, the gift of tongues is not given to facilitate our communication between believers. Most of the time, other people will not understand what you say in tongues—and rightfully so. If the Holy Spirit wants you to communicate with other people, He'll usually give you a prophecy, a word of knowledge or a word of wisdom.

The gift of tongues is a wonderful way to communicate with God. To speak in tongues is to permit the Holy Spirit to pray through you to God the Father. That's why the gift of tongues is often called our *prayer language*.

Besides communicating our prayer needs to God, the Holy Spirit speaks mysteries through us in tongues. In this context, mysteries are not detective puzzles. Mysteries are spiritual truths that are temporarily hidden from human knowledge. God may have a reason for having you pray a certain way to accomplish a special hidden purpose. In due time He may reveal the reason for the prayer, but for now it must remain a mystery.

Medical science tells us that the portion of the brain that controls speech (the cerebral cortex) also controls every other part of the body. Therefore to permit the Holy Spirit to speak through us is to permit Him to affect every part of our lives.

James alluded to this in his epistle, chapter 3 verses 2–4:

> [2] If anyone does not stumble in word, he is a perfect man, able also to bridle the whole body. [3] Indeed, we put bits in horses' mouths that they may obey us, and we turn their whole body. [4] Look also at ships:

although they are so large and are driven by fierce winds, they are turned by a very small rudder wherever the pilot desires. *(MKJV)*

Verses 6–8 continue the thought of our lives being ruled by our tongues:

> [6] And the tongue is a fire, a world of iniquity. The tongue is so set among our members that it defiles the whole body, and sets on fire the course of nature; and it is set on fire by Hell. [7] For every kind of beast and bird, of reptile and creature of the sea, is tamed and has been tamed by mankind. [8] But no man can tame the tongue. It is an unruly evil, full of deadly poison. *(MKJV)*

Note that verse 8 says ". . . no man can tame the tongue." And that is literally true. You and I are not capable of perfectly controlling our tongues for more than a couple of minutes at a time.

That's why the gift of tongues is so profound. If we permit the Holy Spirit to speak through us, we permit God to tame our tongues, at least temporarily.

Returning to 1 Corinthians 14, let's read verses 3–5:

> [3] But he who prophesies speaks edification and exhortation and comfort to men. [4] He who speaks in a tongue edifies himself, but he who prophesies edifies the church. [5] I wish you all spoke with tongues, but even more that you prophesied; for he who prophesies is greater than he who speaks with tongues, unless indeed he interprets, that the church may receive edification. *(NKJV)*

Speaking in tongues, submitting to the leadership of the Holy Spirit, will build you up individually. That is a desirable goal. Paul, however, emphasizes that it is more desirable that we all prophesy, that we may build up each other in the body of Christ.

Verse 5 reintroduces the concept of interpreting tongues. You'll discover that true interpretation is rare, because tongues are generally not given to the edification of the church group.

Tongues is a prayer language, when the Holy Spirit gives you words to pray that you normally don't understand. If the Holy Spirit gives you a prophecy, He will give it to you in a known language and you should speak it as such.

Special note to some friends:

Prayer is supposed to be between you and God. It makes me sad when a person stands up to interpret a message in tongues and begins with the words, "Thus sayeth the Lord . . ." Actually that's a contradiction in terms. Other tongues are a prayer language. Do you normally begin your prayers by saying, "Thus sayeth the Lord . . ." to God? Of course not.

The Hebrew prophets began prophetic messages with the words, "Thus sayeth the Lord." Some modern-day religious folk imagine that they sound more spiritual by saying, "Thus sayeth the Lord." If you say that, please be very careful. God prescribed the death penalty for those who say, "Thus sayeth the Lord" when the Lord has not actually said it.

Likewise, if the Lord gives you a word of prophecy, present it as such. Don't pretend that your word of prophecy is actually an interpretation of somebody else's prayer in tongues. Please set aside your denominational traditions and look at Scripture with fresh eyes. Verses 6–12 give further cautions about speaking in tongues:

> 6 But now, brethren, if I come to you speaking with tongues, what shall I profit you unless I speak to you either by revelation, by knowledge, by prophesying, or by teaching? 7 Even things without life, whether flute or harp, when they make a sound, unless they make a distinction in the sounds, how will it be known what is piped or played? 8 For if the trumpet makes an uncertain sound, who will prepare for battle? 9 So likewise you, unless you utter by the tongue words easy to understand, how will it be known what is spoken? For you will be speaking into the air. 10 There are, it may be, so many kinds of languages in the world, and none of them is without significance. 11 Therefore, if I do not know the meaning of the language, I shall be a foreigner to him who speaks, and he who speaks will be a foreigner to me. 12 Even so you, since you are zealous for spiritual gifts, let it be for the edification of the church that you seek to excel. (*NKJV*)

In Spirit-led worship encounters, many pastors and worship leaders have designated times during the services when people may pray or sing in tongues as a group. This is a wonderful experience when the pastors and leaders have bathed the service in prayer beforehand, and you can sense the love and power working through God's people in their praises.

It is common and normal to feel the Holy Spirit speak through you in tongues. It will usually be a precious, private matter between you and the Lord, even if you feel permission from the Holy Spirit to sing it out loud.

But what if the people standing next to you are first-time visitors? What if the phenomenon of speaking in tongues is new to them? What will they think?

Paul talks about this in verses 13–17:

> [13] Therefore let him who speaks in a tongue pray that he may interpret. [14] For if I pray in a tongue, my spirit prays, but my understanding is unfruitful. [15] What is the conclusion then? I will pray with the spirit, and I will also pray with the understanding. I will sing with the spirit, and I will also sing with the understanding. [16] Otherwise, if you bless with the spirit, how will he who occupies the place of the uninformed say "Amen" at your giving of thanks, since he does not understand what you say? [17] For you indeed give thanks well, but the other is not edified. (*NKJV*)

Another insight: Interpretation need not be an event that interrupts the service to permit the interpreter to speak. In the example above, I might sing a prayer of praise to the Lord in a tongue. Then the Holy Spirit might poke me in the ribs, point to the couple next to me, and give me an interpretation to pray out loud for that couple's benefit. If the other couple is listening, they will be able to say "Amen!" in agreement to the prayer.

Paul says something very interesting in verses 18–20:

> [18] I thank my God I speak with tongues more than you all; [19] yet in the church I would rather speak five words with my understanding, that I may teach others also, than ten thousand words in a tongue. [20] Brethren, do not be children in understanding; however, in malice be babes, but in understanding be mature. (*NKJV*)

Why would Paul write verse 18? Why would it be necessary unless they almost never saw him speak in tongues? Perhaps they *never* saw him speak in tongues.

The implication is that some troublemakers were teaching that Paul wasn't really Spirit-baptized because they had never seen him speak in tongues.

Go back and read the Gospels and count how often Jesus commanded His disciples to speak in tongues. Contrast this with the number of times He commands us to love one another.

Who are the signs for?

Now we come to a brain-bending passage, verses 21 through 22:

> [21] In the law it is written: "With men of other tongues and other lips I will speak to this people; And yet, for all that, they will not hear Me," says the Lord. [22] Therefore tongues are for a sign, not to those who believe but to unbelievers; but prophesying is not for unbelievers but for those who believe. (NKJV)

At first glance, verse 22 appears to contradict everything we've just said. It appears to say that tongues are more helpful to unbelievers rather than believers.

Instead, we should notice that verse 21 is a quotation from Isaiah 28. Isaiah was speaking to his countrymen, fellow Israelites who refused to follow the Lord. Isaiah was predicting that these complacent folks would be conquered by "barbarian" nations; hearing those "barbarian" languages would be a sign that God had judged the godless Israelites. In this case, the unbelieving gentile conquerors would speak unknown tongues to the unbelieving Israelites.

Remember that Jesus often spoke great truths in parables. Everybody heard the words, but most couldn't understand Him. The devoted believers always sought and received an interpretation from Jesus. The casual followers just shrugged and moved along without comprehending.

By contrast, prophecy consists of words inspired by God to be spoken through His believing servants and understood by all the listeners. The listeners will be convicted in their hearts that God has spoken through the prophet(s), and they will respond as believers.

Paul reinforces this concept in verses 23–25:

> [23] Therefore if the whole church comes together in one place, and all speak with tongues, and there come in those who are uninformed or unbelievers, will they not say that you are out of your mind? [24] But if all prophesy, and an unbeliever or an uninformed person comes in, he is convinced by all, he is convicted by all. [25] And thus the secrets of his heart are revealed; and so, falling down on his face, he will worship God and report that God is truly among you. (NKJV)

To summarize this point, in verses 21–23 Paul argues that nonbelievers will continue to be nonbelievers after hearing people speak in tongues. In verses 24–25, Paul declares that nonbelievers are brought under conviction by the Word of God, spoken in prophecy.

Verses 26–33 give practical guidelines for charismatic worship services:

> [26] How is it then, brethren? Whenever you come together, each of you has a psalm, has a teaching, has a tongue, has a revelation, has an interpretation. Let all things be done for edification. [27] If anyone speaks in a tongue, let there be two or at the most three, each in turn, and let one interpret. [28] But if there is no interpreter, let him keep silent in church, and let him speak to himself and to God. [29] Let two or three prophets speak, and let the others judge. [30] But if anything is revealed to another who sits by, let the first keep silent. [31] For you can all prophesy one by one, that all may learn and all may be encouraged. [32] And the spirits of the prophets are subject to the prophets. [33] For God is not the author of confusion but of peace, as in all the churches of the saints. (NKJV)

To repeat, our goal as a community of believers should be to edify the body of Christ. We should seek to strengthen ourselves personally, each other individually, and the group collectively. The latter two goals are foremost in our public worship services. When we gather as the body of Christ, we seek to become strengthened in our submission to Jesus, our Head. We will automatically be strengthened individually when we concentrate on ministering to the Lord and to each other.

Building the body through respect

We must be very careful to respect our brothers and sisters in the Lord. Nothing should be done to showcase or exercise our particular gifts at the expense of others. Every part of the body is valuable and important. Next time you are in a worship service, ask the Holy Spirit to show you how He views the person sitting in the next row: You might be surprised.

Remember that the spirits of the prophets are subject to the prophets. You are not obliged to broadcast a prophetic insight to the group as soon as you receive it. You should ask the Holy Spirit how and when and to whom He would have you deliver the message.

Remember that God is not the author of confusion but of peace. If your congregation is truly submitting to the leadership of the Holy Spirit during worship services, everyone will leave the services feeling blessed, strengthened, and centered in the peace of the Lord.

Are you ready for a little controversy? Try verses 34–36:

[34] Let your women keep silent in the churches, for they are not permitted to speak; but they are to be submissive, as the law also says. [35] And if they want to learn something, let them ask their own husbands at home; for it is shameful for women to speak in church. [36] Or did the word of God come originally from you? Or was it you only that it reached? *(NKJV)*

I've heard women criticize Paul as a *mysogonist* (psychologically imbalanced woman-hater). They are obviously ignorant of the true effect of Paul's writings. In the Greek and Roman cultures, women had no independent rights. Even Jewish men in Paul's day would pray, "I thank you, God, that I am not a Gentile or a woman." Paul was considered a radical feminist in his day by declaring women to be the equals of men.

Paul's epistles are very clear. In God's eyes, we are all equal in value and stature. However, God has ordained that we perform certain roles. God commands men to do the work of priests and kings. The priests and kings are expected to exercise their God-given authority in accordance with God's Law. They will be judged, by God, on how well they conveyed the image of Jesus to those under their authority.

As you have observed by now, men are independent, rebellious, and self-centered by nature. After we men come to the Lord, we are expected to abide in Jesus. God *expects* us to submit to the life-changing work of the Holy Spirit in our hearts.

The Holy Spirit, over time, grows the fruit of the Spirit in our character. Then, and only then, is a man qualified to represent God. Only a humbled, compassionate heart is worthy to serve his congregation as a pastor. Only a humbled, compassionate heart is worthy to serve his wife as a husband. God does not appreciate men who are arrogant and prideful in their exercise of authority.

The point is that God is forever painting pictures for us. God is continually trying to shape men into the image of His Son, Jesus. God's plan is to use broken, submitted, compassionate men to make His love real for us. It truly is a miracle to see a God-fearing, broken, submitted, compassionate man.

Ponder this: It is easier for women, by nature, to be God-fearing and compassionate. That's how God made women. In that respect, it would be easier for God to command women to be pastors because they are seemingly better qualified by nature. Yet that isn't God's plan. God's plan is for every pastor, every husband, every God-humbled teacher to be a walking miracle, and living proof that God is willing and able to change lives.

God's plan is for every man to gain strength and compassion by spending quality time in brokenness before Him.

Women have different responsibilities. They are not inferior in any way. Just different. Women are naturally smarter in relationships and nurturing, and are brilliant at manipulating men to their own devices. That's why only a Spirit-led woman can truly submit to the leadership of a Spirit-led man, and sincerely give the respect that all men urgently need.

Are we off the subject of tongues?

Perhaps. But we're on the general subject of building up the body of Christ, and family units are the core element of the church. It's too easy for men and women to tear down their homes with their tongues, so this little digression is forgivable.

Let's finish with verses 37–40:

> [37] If anyone thinks himself to be a prophet or spiritual, let him acknowledge that the things which I write to you are the commandments of the Lord. [38] But if anyone is ignorant, let him be ignorant. [39] Therefore, brethren, desire earnestly to prophesy, and do not forbid to speak with tongues. [40] Let all things be done decently and in order. (NKJV)

That's pretty clear. "Decently" refers to our relationship with other believers, and "in order" refers to submitting to God's rules. Verse 40, therefore, echoes what Jesus said about the two greatest Commandments.

May the Lord continue to bless you as you study His Word and seek to build up your brothers and sisters in the Lord.

Closing Prayer: Lord, I admit that my behavior in worship has *not* always been according to Your plan. Please change my heart to conform to Your will, and let me truly sing your praises, in tongues of men and angels, for all eternity. Amen!

Chapter 12

Essentials of Prayer

"After this manner, pray ye."

The effectual fervent prayer of a righteous man availeth much. *James 5:16*

Opening Prayer: Father, I don't understand why my prayers have been so lukewarm and ineffective lately. What am I missing? Please bring me to a fresh understanding of Your design for prayer. Amen.

Most of us don't pray enough, do we? As a result, we are often unprepared for the big and little crises that affect us every day. Many times we get hurt because we're unprotected or defenseless.

God has an answer for this problem. He has designed a sophisticated system of defensive and offensive weapons to help us cope with real life. The apostle Paul calls it the "whole armor of God" in his letter to the Ephesians chapter 6, verses 11–18. We've studied this subject in depth in an earlier chapter, but let's re-read a few verses now:

> [11] Put on the whole armor of God so that you may be able to stand against the wiles of the devil. [12] For we do not wrestle against flesh and blood, but against principalities, against powers, against the world's

rulers, of the darkness of this age, against spiritual wickedness in high *places*. [13] Therefore take to yourselves the whole armor of God, that you may be able to withstand in the evil day, and having done all, to stand . . . [18] praying always with all prayer and supplication in the Spirit. (*MKJV*)

Verse 12 is the key. Our key problems in life have a spiritual cause: invisible creatures who influence visible human beings to irrational and violent behavior. Remember what we have learned about the connection between the Scriptures and praying always in the Spirit:

- Reading Scripture makes us aware of God's will. For an unbeliever, this is purely a mental exercise. However, a believer will observe that God's will is to do mighty works in response to prayer.

- Prayer enables us to have fellowship with God, if we pray in accordance with His Word.

- As prayer brings us into God's presence, the Holy Spirit can illuminate the Scriptures and help us understand God's will. The Holy Spirit will help us understand both the general principles and the specific application of His will in our present circumstances.

- Through prayer, we can cling to God's will and become instruments for accomplishing His will here on earth.

Prayer in accordance with God's Word is a powerful weapon. Unlike an arrow or knife, prayer can be launched anywhere from a mobile platform (you!) and change lives anyplace on earth. Think of prayer as the spiritual equivalent of a ballistic missile—one that can *only* be employed to accomplish God's will.

Jesus' disciples observed the many miracles that He worked, and realized that Jesus began His mornings by fortifying Himself in prayer and fellowship with His Father. So they came to Him with a very simple request, as described in Luke 11:

[1] "Lord, teach us to pray."

Doesn't it surprise you that these men were asking such a basic question? After all, they were our Lord's hand-picked disciples. Why did these men—whose greatness has been confirmed by history—feel the need to ask Jesus how to pray?

They asked because they wanted to pray effectively, like Jesus prayed. They knew that Jesus could work miracles through prayer, and they could not. Neither can we, unless we learn to pray like Jesus prayed.

Please don't be intimidated or think prayer involves some elaborate techniques, because it doesn't. Our Lord said we were to come to Him as children, in simplicity of heart. So whatever prayer is, it must be an activity that all believers can participate in, regardless of age or IQ or theological education or physical strength.

Prayer is simple, but most of us underachieve badly in our prayer lives. Much of what the Lord would like to accomplish through our prayers does not get done. We're missing the point somehow. And your teacher has underachieved worse than most.

Let's start our road to recovery by looking at Jesus' answer, in Luke 11:2–4:

> [2] And He said unto them, "When you pray, say, 'Our Father in Heaven, Hallowed be Your Name. Your kingdom come. Your will be done, on earth as *it is* in Heaven. [3] Give us day by day our daily bread. [4] And forgive us our sins; for we also forgive every one that is indebted to us. And lead us not into temptation; but deliver us from the evil one.'" *(NKJV)*

This prayer should look very familiar to you. Many of us grew up reciting this prayer, with slight wording variations. In fact, most of us let its familiarity blind us to its profound truth.

Notice that Jesus has structured this prayer according to the pattern expressed in Matthew chapter 6:

> [33] But seek ye first the kingdom of God, and His righteousness, and all these things shall be added unto you.

This seems really backwards. It doesn't feel right to pay more attention to an invisible God than to our visible problems. Our pressing physical and emotional needs drive us to our knees and we want to immediately start praying for relief. Why should we stop and pray for all this spiritual stuff first?

Because it is not just "spiritual stuff." It's the key element in the prayer itself. We can (and do) talk endlessly about ourselves and our wants and needs, but that's not prayer. Prayer is dialogue with God Himself, to achieve purposes unattainable in our own strength. Since He is God, He has a right to establish the terms. Fortunately for us, He has made the terms fairly simple.

Remember, too, that this model prayer represents God's will for our life. Whatever He asks us to pray for must be something He wants us to have.

So let's take the prayer, phrase by phrase, and see how it forms the outline of all effective prayers.

Our Father in Heaven . . .

First, prayer must be directed to a specific Recipient. Our Lord makes it clear that we are to pray to God the Father. Yes, we can occasionally say devotional prayers of gratitude and thanksgiving to Jesus and the Holy Spirit. But we are commanded to direct our normal prayer to God the Father.

Please note that Jesus could have called Him "God-the-Boss" or "God-the-Only-One-Whose-Opinion-Matters." Instead, we are to call Him "Father"—the One Who knows and cares about us more than anyone else.

We can only call Him "Father" if we have a personal relationship with Him, as described in the earlier chapters of this book. We must surrender to Jesus as Savior and Lord before receiving the blessings of God, our Father.

Second, the Recipient has a specific address: in Heaven. Wherever Heaven is, it's quite different from here. And God the Father is completely and visibly and wonderfully in charge. There are no theological debates in Heaven. There is only one God, and His presence is real and unmistakable. Our Father in Heaven is all-powerful and capable of doing whatever He wills.

Hallowed be Your Name

Everyone in the Scriptures who encountered God had the same reaction: they were overwhelmed by the majesty and power and holiness of God. The "Name" of God represents all of that.

So after we identify the proper Recipient of prayer, we focus on His character and His Name. We begin with praise for our Father.

Praise is the very foundation of effective prayer. Like the Psalm writers, we praise God for His power, His wisdom, His love, His mercy and His grace. We thank God for the many blessings we receive each day, and for the incredible beauty of His creation.

Hint: Reading the Psalms out loud is a good way to get started. Praising God with your audible voice will help tune your whole body to the truth of God's love for you.

Your kingdom come, . . .

If we've done it right so far, we become conscious of the vast difference between God and us. As we remember and praise God for the ways He has provided for us, we see what a good and gracious King He really is.

Now let's remember that a kingdom is an area ruled by a king. Does He rule in my heart? Have I ever submitted to God and surrendered authority over my life to Him? Have I ever made a conscious decision to acknowledge His Son—Jesus, Yeshua—as my Lord and Savior?

Do I take up my cross daily and open my heart in submission to the gentle leading of the Holy Spirit in my life? Or am I governed by my passions, self will, family and friends?

God has a Kingdom and exactly one simple plan for qualifying to participate in that Kingdom. We must trust completely in the redeeming sacrifice of His Son, Jesus, on Calvary. As we saw earlier, we surely can't earn our salvation by our own good works.

. . . Your will be done, on earth as it is in Heaven.

Are you with the program so far? Congratulations. You've acknowledged the God of Abraham, Isaac and Jacob as God of your life, and you've surrendered to the Lordship of His Son and the daily infilling and leading of the Holy Spirit. Now comes the most difficult part: requesting that God's will be done.

Please don't underestimate this part. Some days, it is difficult to believe that God is really in control of our circumstances. Like a television drama, there are horrible problems and obstacles, but the Good Guy will win. And those of us who trust in Jesus will live happily forever after with Him.

Some days, the "happily forever after" part is hard to believe. We're really hurting, right now. Our problems have already arrived, and it feels like they'll never be solved. We mentally understand God's promises, but they seem far away in the distant future.

God's will requires us to take a long-range perspective. Certainly nothing we've experienced on earth can compare to the glory of God, and He wants us to be face-to-face with Him, experiencing that glory.

His glory is incomparable, and it's forever. No earthly mansion can compare to where you and I will live for eternity. The question is, will we trust Him and cooperate with His plan until we get there?

His plan includes difficult times. His way involves sacrifice. His will is for you to be purified, strengthened and empowered by His Spirit. His plan calls for changes in your life, to prepare you for participation in His life.

This is not a matter of giving up *bad* stuff. The Holy Spirit calls us to give up *our* stuff. Two wills cannot exist in the same body. We cannot serve God and self. Self is very deceptive:

- Self can lead us to do great and wonderful things in the name of God—things that God didn't ask us to do.

- Self can teach and preach and build churches that God didn't ask us to build.

- Self can appear to conform to written Word of God, without submitting to the Spirit of God.

- Self can be as subtle and beguiling as the serpent in the Garden, and just as harmful.

- Self is an enemy of God. Don't listen to its pitiful cries; it must go to the cross.

When we pray, "Your will be done . . ." we acknowledge that God's plan might be different from ours. It might inconvenience us terribly. It might cost us time and money. It might cost us our lives. But we choose to listen to God's plan and to move, in faith, in that direction.

At times, the Lord wants us to be His agents for accomplishing His will. He will bring a particular promise to our hearts and give us a burning passion for it. For example, the prophet Isaiah wrote down many of the Lord's extravagant promises to Israel in chapters 60 through 66 of the book that bears his name.

Some of the promises have already been fulfilled through Israel's return to their homeland, but some remain future. We know they must be God's will, but God commands that we pray these promises into existence down here, on earth. We see this in Isaiah chapter 62:

> ⁶ I have set watchmen upon thy walls, O Jerusalem, who shall never hold their peace day nor night: ye that make mention of the LORD,

keep not silence, [7] And give Him no rest, till He establish, and till he make Jerusalem a praise in the earth.

As you grow in the Lord and dwell longer in prayer, the Holy Spirit will speak to your heart. He will make His promises in Scripture real to your heart. Then He will ask you to labor over these promises, as a mother giving birth to a child. He will ask you to ". . . give Him no rest, till . . ." the Father makes good on His promises.

God's will for you is good. He is faithful to His promises. We must open our eyes to read and understand His Word, the sword of the Spirit. Then we must let the Holy Spirit of God work through us, in prayer, to accomplish His will.

Give us day by day our daily bread . . .

Finally we get to familiar ground. We've never seen Heaven, but we know all about bread.

Now we can pray about what we want. And look at the irony of the situation: we've just asked God for His will to be done. We've given away the store! We've given away all our negotiating leverage!

Now all we can possibly get is what God wants to give us! Is that such a bad thing?

Remember: there is nothing in this model prayer except what God wants us to have. So notice how the first thing the Lord wants us to have is enough. We are commanded to pray for our necessities, with the understanding that we will receive them, day by day.

As we read in Psalm 23:

[2] He makes me to lie down in green pastures; He leads me beside still waters. (*MKJV*)

God promises to give us enough to eat and drink. He promises green pastures, not barns full of hay.

And forgive us our sins; for we also forgive every one that is indebted to us.

Here's another biggie. How many people do you know that harbor unforgiveness? They've been hurt. They have a right to be angry, and they are. And this resentment (often buried deep and disguised as something else) is ruining their lives and health.

Unforgiveness is a dangerous form of heart disease. Undiagnosed and uncorrected, it will cause physical and emotional disability. Worse, it can disqualify us from Heaven.

The apostle Peter wrestled with the issue of forgiveness in Matthew 18, verses 21–22:

> [21] Then Peter came to Him and said, "Lord, how often shall my brother sin against me and I forgive him? Until seven times?" [22] Jesus said to him, "I do not say to you, 'Until seven times;' but, 'Until seventy times seven.'" *(MKJV)*

Peter surely thought Jesus would be impressed by Peter's willingness to forgive a person seven times. So Peter must have been floored by Jesus' response, that we should forgive a person up to 490 times.

Actually, 490 times makes sense. Let's say that you forgive a person today, and feel at peace about the subject now. But if it was a serious matter, your conscious mind will probably touch on that subject an additional 490 times in the course of your lifetime. You must resolve in your heart now to give up your "right" to be angry about this for the upcoming 489 remembrances.

Some folks wonder whether we should pray "Forgive us our trespasses" or "Forgive us our debts." Why waste time wondering? Both are valid. Confess your sins, confess your unforgiveness, learn of God's grace and forgiveness, and receive peace and forgiveness for yourself.

And lead us not into temptation; but deliver us from evil.

Does God tempt us to sin? Obviously not. He doesn't need to. We have more temptation than we can handle from just our flesh and from the enemy of our souls.

God has a special blessing in view. When we become "born again," the Holy Spirit comes to dwell in our hearts and give us new life. God's Holy Spirit can give us the strength to endure times of trial and testing.

He can give us power and wisdom to be delivered from the crushing desires of our own flesh. He can give us power and wisdom to avoid the traps of the evil one.

The nastiest trap is self pity. You've heard the evil one's lies before: "You're no good. You'll never be good enough. You'll never qualify for Heaven, because you'll never amount to anything. You can't even be successful in *this* world, so what makes you think any of God's promises apply to you? Why don't you just give up now and be done with it?"

Don't listen to that stuff. It's temptation. If you focus on yourself, you'll become hyper-sensitive to your own failings.

Focus on Jesus instead. He already paid the price for your salvation. He has already redeemed you from what you really deserve. His Word is true, and His Holy Spirit—dwelling in your heart—is His part payment of your eternal inheritance.

Focus on Jesus, and fill your mind and heart with His Word. Lift your hands and voice in praise, and don't make room in your life for temptation.

For Thine is the kingdom and the power and the glory, forever.

Matthew's account of the model prayer (apparently given on a different occasion) ends with this doxology. It illustrates an important point: Prayer should begin and end with praise to God. Not because God is insecure and needs affirmation. We should praise God because we need to do so.

If we can sincerely praise God in the midst of great difficulty, it's an act of faith that can open the gates of Heaven on our behalf. Praising God is acknowledging that we trust Him regardless of our circumstances. It drives away fear and makes the Enemy cover his ears and flee.

In case you have any doubts about the power of praise, try a science experiment: spend an hour alone, praising God with all your heart for everything you can think of. It will change your life.

Amen

These words of Jesus are simple enough for a child to remember. But please don't settle for just the words. Open your heart to the Lord, and spend quality time with Him. Seek His presence, and settle for nothing less.

Practical Application

History tells us that James, our Lord's half-brother, was a mighty man of prayer. We can see this in his general epistle, chapter 5:

> [13] Is any among you afflicted? Let him pray. Is any merry? Let him sing psalms. [14] Is any sick among you? Let him call for the elders of the church; and let them pray over him, anointing him with oil in the name of the Lord. [15] And the prayer of faith shall save the sick, and the Lord shall raise him up; and if he has committed sins, they shall be forgiven him.

In just three verses, James manages to connect prayer to every aspect of human life:

- **Affliction.** We can seldom go more than a week without being thumped by "life" in some area. James has a simple answer: drop to your knees and pray for God to restore your *panoply* (full armor of God). Spend time in prayer and Bible study, to reestablish your focus on God's character and His promises. As you abide in the Holy Spirit, searching the Scriptures, He will guide you to the way of escape.

- **Good Times.** Admit it: most of us relax and drop our defenses when the good times arrive. We get comfortable. We forget that our enemy is being temporarily restrained by God's power. We forget to give God the glory for His grace and protection. But we shouldn't. When the happy times arrive, we should spend extra time in prayer, reading the psalms aloud and praising God for His faithfulness. Play your CDs and tapes of praise music in your car on the way to work. Tell your family and friends that God has blessed you in a wonderful way.

- **Sickness.** Some days our bodies really feel like they're made from the dust of the earth. We feel beaten down physically and emotionally. James recommends that we call on our brothers and sisters in our church fellowship for prayer, and for anointing with oil. Please note that he is not calling for Christians to carry around bottles of olive oil. In those days, various types of anointing oils were used as medication. James is actually telling us to combine sensible medical care with therapeutic prayer.

- **Faith.** As we study the Scriptures and pray for wisdom, the Holy Spirit will often quicken a particular passage to our attention. Likewise, when we hear prayer requests, the Holy Spirit often gives us insight into the Lord's will for a person or situation. If we have correctly discerned His will, and if we act in faith on it, His own power will bring His will to pass. The sick will be healed. The impossible will be accomplished. The sinner will be converted.

We obtain even more insights from the next three verses of James chapter 5:

> [16] Confess your faults one to another, and pray one for another, that ye may be healed. The effectual fervent prayer of a righteous man availeth much. [17] Elias was a man subject to like passions as we are, and he prayed earnestly that it might not rain: and it rained not on the earth by the space of three years and six months. [18] And he prayed again, and the heaven gave rain, and the earth brought forth her fruit.

These verses are more difficult and more backwards than the previous ones. They describe activities that are definitely uncomfortable for people who haven't experienced the fullness of the Holy Spirit:

- **Forgiveness of sins.** We all sin and come short of the glory of God. James exhorts us to confess our faults to God in prayer, as directed in 1 John chapter one, verse 9: "If we confess our sins, He is faithful and just to forgive us our sins and cleanse us from all unrighteousness." If we have sinned against a particular brother or sister, we are called to confess to that person and ask for forgiveness.

- **Fervency in prayer.** Nothing in our flesh will help us develop a fervent passion for prayer. We seem to get very excited about athletic contests and entertainment events, but how many of us quickly grasp the concept of burning passion in prayer? Challenge your own heart in this regard. If you would be more excited about meeting a movie star than encountering the Creator of the universe in prayer, then get on your knees right now and ask God for forgiveness.

- **Miracles**. God doesn't ask very many people to pray for drought or for rain. But if He wanted to bring drought to your community or to your place of employment, would God ask you to do the praying? Would you be willing to pray, in faith, for God to bring judgment there? Do you have the faith to act in faith on His request, despite the risk of personal loss or injury?

Much of what God wants to do in your life might seem impossible today, but you can trust God to fully prepare and equip you. Just remember that the Bible and prayer must travel together as a team. First, pray for the Holy Spirit to quicken your understanding as you read the Bible. Then be receptive to His leading.

Some day, you'll come to the end of your dignified prayer. Some day, you will experience true brokenness in prayer, and discover the sweet love and power that awaits you behind the veil. If you have never experienced this blessed type of prayer, be sure to read the next chapter, "Brokenness." You have a treat coming.

Closing Prayer: Our Father in Heaven, we praise You for Your love and grace toward us. Forgive us of our lukewarm prayers. Show us what it means to be Your children, walking in obedience to Your will, living in the peace and joy that can only come from Your hand. May Your will be done in our lives, and may your Holy Spirit guide us into sweet communion with You, we pray. Amen.

Chapter 13

Brokenness

Have I missed God somehow?

So she, having been prompted by her mother, said, "Give me John the Baptist's head here on a platter." *Matthew 14:8*

Opening Prayer: Lord, some days, it looks like the Bad Guys are winning. I've done my best, but now somebody with power is asking for my head on a platter. Lord, help me to have your perspective so I can make it through this time of distress. Amen.

*D*uring the past year, several of my friends lost their jobs or had their businesses fail as the economy weakened. Some of these friends are Christians, with sharp minds and great personal integrity. They worked long and hard, but have little or nothing to show for it.

Some friends of mine are experiencing tremendous physical pain: cancer, rheumatoid arthritis and fibromyalgia. Others are trying to recover from broken marriages or relationships.

All of these are painful and cause our hearts to grieve. We feel broken, discarded.

Does that sound like you? Congratulations. You qualify for the greatest power in prayer. If your heart can get empty enough, the Holy Spirit can fill you with mountain-moving power.

Painfully Backwards

This is yet another lesson in how the Kingdom of God is upside-down and backwards compared to what we knew in the world. But it's consistent with the other lessons you've learned so far:

- You realize that you've spent all your life in a battlefield, getting attacked by a hateful, invisible enemy who wants to destroy you.

- You have decided to take action by receiving salvation as a free gift from Jesus, the Messiah of Israel, who paid a terrible price to purchase it for you.

- You have been baptized in water and with the Holy Spirit.

- You have resigned your position in the devil's army and have enlisted in God's Army.

- You have been given the weapons of our warfare: the gifts of the Holy Spirit and the *panoply* (whole armor) of God.

- You have learned that your fellow soldiers (the B-Team) are a pretty odd-looking group.

Now you're engaged in spiritual warfare. You didn't *ask* to get involved, but the Lord has permitted it.

By now, you probably suspect there's something backwards about warfare, too. And you're right. God has established an absolutely crazy way to get you pumped up for battle: by grinding you into the dust.

Truth #1: God will let you fail.

There's an important lesson to be learned from the life of David. God had chosen David to be the next king of Israel. God had empowered David to slay the giant and to lead the armies of Israel to many great victories.

David had achieved great success and fame. Everybody loved him—except King Saul and a few people who bore personal grudges. Saul was actively chasing David to kill him, so David fled the country, seeking refuge among the Philistines.

We read the story in 1 Samuel 21:

[10] Then David arose and fled that day from before Saul, and went to Achish the king of Gath. [11] And the servants of Achish said to him, "Is this not David the king of the land? Did they not sing of him to one another in dances, saying: 'Saul has slain his thousands, And David his ten thousands'?" [12] Now David took these words to heart, and was very much afraid of Achish the king of Gath. [13] So he changed his behavior before them, feigned madness in their hands, scratched on the doors of the gate, and let his saliva fall down on his beard. [14] Then Achish said to his servants, "Look, you see the man is insane. Why have you brought him to me? [15] "Have I need of madmen, that you have brought this fellow to play the madman in my presence? Shall this fellow come into my house?" *(NKJV)*

Truth #2: Not only will you fail, but you probably will look bad in the process.

David "succeeded" in escaping the Philistines by pretending to be a madman. But how do you suppose he felt afterwards? Had he missed God somewhere along the way? Was it God's will for David to act crazy? Was it God's will for Saul to be chasing him? What will people think of David after this little scene? Would he live long enough to be the next king?

Fortunately, we don't have to guess at David's reaction. He recorded his thoughts and feelings in Psalm 34, so we could see how a God-fearing warrior copes with hardship. Let's start with the first three verses:

[1] I will bless the Lord at all times; His praise shall continually be in my mouth. [2] My soul shall make its boast in the Lord; The humble shall hear of it and be glad. [3] Oh, magnify the Lord with me, And let us exalt His name together. *(NKJV)*

At first glance, you'd never guess that David was experiencing bitter failure, alone in a cave in enemy territory. In fact, you could read these verses aloud in Church and nobody would have a clue about the writer's circumstances.

Truth #3: Stay focused on God, His faithfulness and His character.

We get our first hint of backwards warfare in verse 2 above: "My soul shall make its boast in the Lord; The humble shall hear of it and be glad."

David had lost everything at this point. He had been chased out of his home, out of his country, and had to humiliate himself to keep from being imprisoned by Achish, the Philistine king. David had no money, no land, no army, no prestige.

All he had left was his relationship with God. That was enough to make David break out singing praises to God. Was David a nut case or did he see beyond his circumstances?

David knew that God had made promises to him, and those promises were more real to David than the threats of King Saul. God's promises were real, because God's character is faithful.

God has made promises to you, too. Your promises might be less dramatic than David's, but they could be huge nonetheless. God will keep every one of those promises, even if the process of claiming these promises could be painful.

Pay attention, now. David begins to give instructions for spiritual warfare in verses 4 and 6 of Psalm 34:

> [4] I sought the Lord, and He heard me, and delivered me from all my fears. [6] This poor man cried out, and the Lord heard him, and saved him out of all his troubles. (*NKJV*)

Notice that God has sharply divided battlefield responsibilities. Your job is to seek the Lord and cry out to Him. God's job is to hear you, deliver you from your fears and save you from all your troubles.

Would you rather have it the worldly way? Picture how the United States conducts war. The Commander in Chief (the President) confers with his military advisors and determines policy and strategy. Then his military generals send orders down a long chain of command to the troops (you!) to break camp and attack the enemy.

That's the worldly way. The worldly way would have God calling out to you, like Commissioner Gordon calling Batman, and having *you* ride out and fix the problem.

God's way is backwards. An individual soldier cries out directly to the Commander in Chief of the Entire Universe. Then the Commander in Chief of the Entire Universe bends the rules of all creation in order to rescue you from the enemy.

Would you rather have the warfare depend on *your* strength? Would you trust your future to that? Neither would I.

Let's continue in Psalm 34, with verses 15–16:

> [15] The eyes of the Lord are on the righteous, And His ears are open to their cry. [16] The face of the Lord is against those who do evil, To cut off the remembrance of them from the earth. *(NKJV)*

For the umteenth time, God is telling you to trust Him. His character is good and faithful. He is constantly attending to the righteous folks (those who have taken advantage of the Big Loophole), and His ears are open to their cries.

By contrast, He is very hostile to His enemies. When you pray for God's will and against evildoers, You can be sure God is listening to your prayers and leaning your direction.

Now for three verses, 17 through 19, that really sum up the power of brokenness:

> [17] The righteous cry out, and the Lord hears, And delivers them out of all their troubles. [18] The Lord is near to those who have a broken heart, And saves such as have a contrite spirit. [19] Many are the afflictions of the righteous, But the Lord delivers him out of them all. *(NKJV)*

Truth #4: Weeping is a powerful weapon.

Face it: if you are righteous, you will have many afflictions. Hardship will break your heart and drive you face-down into the dirt. You will have no strength to fight. You will barely be able to raise your voice to cry out to God for help.

Fortunately, that's all it takes. If you have given your heart to the Lord, the Lord knows when your heart is broken. When you are so broken that you give up even the illusion of strength, God can help you.

When trauma strikes, cry out to God. Cling like a drowning person to the promises of Scripture and the character of God. Give up your pride and your façade of self-sufficiency. Confess that your strength is not sufficient to handle the hardship. Let the Holy Spirit break your heart.

In the middle of that weeping and brokenness, the Holy Spirit will do a work. God Himself will be moved with compassion. The power that created the universe is now fully tuned in to you and your problems.

Truth #5: Be sure you're confessed up.

Notice that verse 18 says that God saves those who have a contrite heart, who repent and turn away from their fleshly failings. Romans 3:23 says that all have sinned and come short of the glory of God. "All" translates a Greek word *pas* that means "all." It includes you and me. If you can't think of any ways that you have sinned or come short of God's glory, then get on your knees and repent of your pride.

Most of us, though, are painfully aware of our shortcomings. We're aware of the little weaknesses and habits that distract our hearts from the Lord. You are probably aware of your tendency to anger or to impurity or to gossip. Confess it and let the Lord take it from you. That tendency can put invisible handlebars on your heart, and make it easy for the devil to steer you around like a kid's scooter, right into trouble.

Major unconfessed sin can make you more dangerous than a hijacked scooter. Maybe you're fond of extra-marital sex, substance abuse, pornography, or some other life-wasting habit. Give it up. Being "under the influence of" one of these practices makes you more like a hijacked airliner—unless you give control of your life back to the Lord, you'll crash and burn and hurt lots of innocent people.

Your favorite sins have already caused you enough pain and grief. Don't let them cheat you out of the wonderful blessings of being in the Lord's will and in His mighty presence. Even "little" sins can cripple your walk, if you don't repent and confess them.

Remember the words of 1 John chapter 1 verse 9:

> If we confess our sins, He is faithful and just to forgive us *our* sins, and to cleanse us from all unrighteousness.

Confess your faults, your pride and your self sufficiency. Then cry your way through *everything* about the original problem (which drove you to prayer in the first place) and turn *everything* over to God.

When you have utterly come to the end of your strength and pride, God will pry the problem out of your hands and start fighting for you.

The first thing he will touch is your heart. At some point in your crying, you'll feel the burden lift. The crying will stop. You feel peace.

Your mind will object that your circumstances haven't changed and that God hasn't done anything yet. Your mind is wrong, because the Lord's power has already worked one miracle: He's given you peace.

Paul describes this as the "peace of God, which surpasses all understanding." (Philippians 4:6) You won't be able to understand it, but you can surely be grateful for it.

Truth #6: Peace is a miracle. Be grateful for it.

When the burden lifts, you'll probably still feel pretty weak and fragile, but move forward in faith. Let God lead you. He will resolve your situation His way, and He'll bring an answer according to His own timetable, which is always different from yours.

Truth #7: Faith involves moving forward when God directs, even before your eyes see all the answers.

Your mind will drive you crazy, running over all the details that aren't cleaned up and fixed yet. Your mouth will tempt you to sin by asking why hasn't God given you a satisfactory answer to This, That or The Other Thing. "What am I going to do? God knows that I need This!"

Just remember that God is pretty smart. He won't waste His time giving you a false sense of peace and safety. If He gives you peace and direction, walk boldly right where He shows you.

Painful Plantings

True confession time: this author is a low-energy guy. Much of the time, I don't feel capable of doing God's work. After work, I often don't have the time or strength or will to do anything constructive.

But God has other tasks in mind for me—to minister to my family, to my friends or to the visitors who read the material on my various ministry web sites. In recent months, there has been the work of book publishing.

My flesh is tempted to say, "I can't do this, Lord. I just can't spare another ounce of energy tonight!"

We've all felt like that, but still the Lord will say, "But what about my dear children Charles and Wanda next door? They would love to have you drop by and share encouragement from Scripture! And what about Mary, who just poured out her heart in an e-mail, seeking any word of hope from Me? I'll give you strength to minister to them, I promise."

God's work is impossible in our own strength, so we must lean on His strength. He gives us some clear guidance in Psalm 126, verses 5 and 6:

⁵ Those who sow in tears shall reap in joy. ⁶ He who continually goes forth weeping, bearing seed for sowing, shall doubtless come again with rejoicing, bringing his sheaves with him. *(NKJV)*

Were you raised on a farm? Neither was I. But this passage speaks volumes to men like my father, who was raised on a dirt farm in North Dakota. Every winter, a portion of the grain harvest had to be reserved as seed for the next crop of wheat. If the harvest had been small, the seed represented a larger portion of the family's livelihood. Planting the full measure of seed was an act of faith, because this same grain could be sold for cash or ground up to make bread to feed the family.

Some years it was painful to plant the full measure of seed, knowing there would be several lean months before harvest, which was never guaranteed. Likewise God calls us to step out in faith for Him even when we're heartbroken ourselves.

A wheat harvest is never assured. But Jesus promises to give us treasures in Heaven, where rust and moths and terrorists cannot destroy them. The rewards of our faith will be like the farmers' precious sheaves, and we will rejoice in time if we persevere.

God is faithful. His promises are trustworthy. His harvest of blessings for you is assured.

Closing Prayer: Lord, I understand the broken feeling, but I haven't yet gained complete confidence in victory through Your Holy Spirit. Change my heart to see the wisdom and truth in Your difficult way, I pray in Jesus' name. Amen.

Chapter 14

Boldness

Perfect Love Casts Out Fear

> Yea, though I walk through the valley of the shadow of death, I will fear no evil: for Thou art with me; Thy rod and Thy staff they comfort me. *Psalm 23:4*

Opening Prayer: Father, it gets pretty dark down here sometimes. But I know that You are with me, even through the worst valleys. Comfort me and give me courage to move forward in faith, I pray. Amen.

*H*ave you ever walked through the valley of the shadow of death? Of course you have. Sometimes that valley contained the shadow of physical death, for you or a loved one. Perhaps you experienced terrible injury, illness, or failure of a relationship.

Our Lord, the Great Shepherd, calls us to walk boldly through this dreadful valley. This will truly prove the durability of the joy that God has birthed in your heart.

Two backwards truths

Most worldly boldness is based on feelings of personal strength and competence. A professional athlete boldly approaches competition, knowing that he or she has the personal gifts and training to achieve great performance. God calls us to be bold for reasons that seem backward to human logic:

- Although we are weak and vulnerable, we can trust an invisible God to protect us because His faithfulness and His love for us.

- Although we despise the dark valley, it is often the shortest path to places of great joy and peace.

God's plan calls for a change in your heart. He wants you to discern between healthy fear and unhealthy fear. He also wants you to respond in faith when our enemy tries to discourage you from following Jesus. The key is understanding the character and faithfulness of our Lord.

Healthy Fear

When I was a boy walking with my earthly dad, nobody (except him) could touch me. My only fear was a healthy fear of displeasing my dad. I knew my dad loved me and would take care of me.

Jesus applied this principle to His eternal Father in Matthew 10, verses 28–31:

> [28] And fear not them which kill the body, but are not able to kill the soul: but rather fear him which is able to destroy both soul and body in Hell. [29] Are not two sparrows sold for a farthing? and one of them shall not fall on the ground without your Father. [30] But the very hairs of your head are all numbered. [31] Fear ye not therefore, ye are of more value than many sparrows.

Strange as it sounds, fear is a gift from God. Fear is a normal, human response to a situation or person that could harm us. Growing up, we learn healthy fear of fire, heights, poisonous snakes, and playing in the street.

Here is another backwards truth about Christianity: Healthy fear will enable us to overcome the fears that our enemies try to use as weapons against us.

Healthy fear defines our safe boundaries. We instinctively stop when we encounter a dangerous situation or person.

By contrast, unhealthy fear can stop us from making any type of progress in life. Our enemies strive to gain their goals by striking fear into our hearts. God wants to give us the wisdom and boldness to rightly discern healthy from unhealthy fear.

Healthy fear is an essential part of maturity. The most difficult fear to learn is fear of proper authority. We are all born rebels, self-centered and impatient. We resent being ordered around, especially by those who appear to enjoy it. We take perverted pleasure in escaping the consequences of our secret violations of the rules.

Unfortunately, the most obvious target to rebel against is God. The easiest rules to violate are God's commandments in the Bible. And it seems like we never get caught and punished for seemingly harmless violations like coveting other folks' property or spouses.

Our generation has lost its healthy fear of God. We have grown up watching celebrities in movies and TV break all the moral rules and get rich in the process. But are they really getting away with anything? Do you really think God ignores or approves of rebellion?

The book of Proverbs is mainly concerned with God-fearing wisdom. In the very first chapter, Solomon shows the powerful contrast between the foolish and the wise:

> [7] The fear of the LORD is the beginning of knowledge: but fools despise wisdom and instruction.

Wisdom is intelligently applied knowledge. We need knowledge before we can start gaining wisdom, and the fear of the Lord is the very first thing we must learn as we acquire knowledge.

God freely offers to teach us, but our sinful natures struggle against Him. Proverbs 1, verses 23 through 29 tell a sad (but familiar) story:

> [23] Turn you at my reproof: behold, I will pour out My Spirit unto you, I will make known My words unto you. [24] Because I have called, and ye refused; I have stretched out My hand, and no man regarded; [25] But ye have set at nought all My counsel, and would none of My reproof: [26] I also will laugh at your calamity; I will mock when your fear cometh; [27] When your fear cometh as desolation, and your destruction cometh as a whirlwind; when distress and anguish cometh upon you. [28] Then shall they call upon Me, but I will not answer; they shall seek Me

early, but they shall not find Me: [29] For that they hated knowledge, and did not choose the fear of the LORD.

If we accept His knowledge and learn healthy fear of His power, we will grow stronger and wiser. God promises to strengthen and encourage us. But if we get comfortable in our rebellion against Him, He is under no obligation to bail us out when trouble strikes.

Psalm 110 verse 10 shows that we should pay close attention to what God expects from us:

[10] The fear of the LORD is the beginning of wisdom: a good understanding have all they that do his commandments: his praise endureth for ever.

Overcoming Fear through Faith

Now that we have learned about healthy fear, we can talk about our enemy's tactics. Our enemy loves to work behind the scenes, using political and religious "terrorists" to attack us. These misguided human zealots are not our enemy, as we remember from Ephesians 6:12, which says:

[12] For we wrestle not against flesh and blood, but against principalities, against powers, against the rulers of the darkness of this world, against spiritual wickedness in the heavenly places.

The evil, invisible "rulers of the darkness" are much more powerful than we are in our human nature. However, our heavenly Father is infinitely more powerful than all these rulers combined. If our heavenly Father can be trusted, then we should seek His protection. We should position ourselves very near to Him.

Positioning yourself near Him is the same as abiding in our Lord Jesus Christ, as we saw in an earlier chapter. When you abide in the written word of God, and spend quality time in prayer with the Living Word, you will come to understand the character and faithfulness of God. You will know, by personal experience, that God loves you.

When you know that God loves you, and you are actively abiding in His love, the terrorists cannot make you fearful. The Apostle John, famous for his loving relationship with Jesus, expresses this truth in his first epistle, chapter 4:

[16] And we have known and believed the love that God has in us. God is love, and he who abides in love abides in God, and God in him. [17] In this is our love made perfect, that we may have boldness in the day of judgment, that as He is, so also we are in this world. [18] There is no fear in love, but **perfect love casts out fear**, because fear has torment. He who fears has not been perfected in love. [19] We love Him because He first loved us. (MKJV)

Please pay special attention to verse 18: "There is no fear in love, but perfect love casts out fear." When you are truly in love with God and abiding in His Son, Jesus, you will be filled with His love. His love will displace your unhealthy fears.

Perhaps your physical dad was not as caring and strong as mine, so maybe it's difficult for you to directly relate to this feeling. Then let me encourage you to move out in faith to earnestly seek this relationship with Jesus and His Father.

When you spend the quality time with Jesus and the Scriptures, you will become convinced of His faithfulness and His love for you. You can trust a God like ours. His love will give you courage to face the inevitable hard times.

Hard times

When somebody asks, "How could a good God allow . . . ?" I have two standard responses. The first response is explained in the next chapter, "Blessings." The second response takes the form of a question, "How could a good God allow professional football?"

Don't laugh. Think about what a professional football player must endure:

- A childhood that includes being pushed and tackled by the biggest kids in town, plus endless amounts of verbal abuse from coaches and opponents.
- High school and college years filled with grueling physical work and painful injuries.
- Having the biggest and fastest athletes in the world knock you down (or unconscious) all day long.
- An extremely short working lifetime, typically less than 7 years and frequently ended by a crippling injury or concussion(s).
- A "retirement" haunted by physical pain and often an early death.

So why play professional football? Your immediate response is probably: "For the rewards! The money! The glory! The excitement!"

God allows us to suffer for the same reason: for the rewards. The apostle Paul puts it very neatly in his second letter to the Corinthians, chapter 4 verses 15–18:

> [15] For all things *are* for your sakes, that the abundant grace might through the thanksgiving of many redound to the glory of God. [16] For which cause we faint not; but though our outward man perish, yet the inward *man* is renewed day by day. [17] For our light affliction, which is but for a moment, worketh for us a far more exceeding *and* eternal weight of glory; [18] While we look not at the things which are seen, but at the things which are not seen: for the things which are seen *are* temporal; but the things which are not seen *are* eternal.

Paul begins this outrageous passage by saying the dark valley is good for you (verse 15) and that we even though our human lives are whipped and torn (verse 16), our inward character can be renewed day by day.

Then he has the nerve to call your problems "light affliction." Of course, he had the right to say that. For him, the walk of faith included being stoned by hostile mobs, being whipped by Roman torturers, being shipwrecked, and being beaten by religious fanatics. If Paul can call his problems "light," I shouldn't be too fearful of mine.

It's wrong to think that only great heroes of faith can endure suffering boldly. On the contrary, enduring suffering boldly makes great heroes of faith out of ordinary men and women.

If God's promises are true, then we have much to gain from the difficult times, as we'll see in the next chapter.

Love: An Action Verb

God's love gives us boldness, but not if we receive it passively. We must respond to God's love in faith, so the Holy Spirit can produce the fruit of love in our hearts.

When we first begin to grasp God's love, we're blinded by its power and brilliance. We're stunned, wondering what to do next. Then, as His love is poured into our hearts, we feel compelled to share it with a world that desperately needs it.

Remember the words of Jesus in Matthew 7, verses 16–17:

¹⁶ You shall know them by their fruits. Do men gather grapes from thorns, or figs from thistles? ¹⁷ Even so every good tree brings forth good fruit; but a corrupt tree brings forth evil fruit. *(MKJV)*

As we abide in Jesus, spending quality time with Him in Bible study and prayer, He plants His love in our hearts and makes us fruitful in Him.

The apostle Paul expressed it beautifully in his first letter to the Corinthians, chapter 13:

¹ Though I speak with the tongues of men and of angels, and have not love, I am become as sounding brass, or a tinkling cymbal. ² And though I have the gift of prophecy, and understand all mysteries, and all knowledge; and though I have all faith, so that I could remove mountains, and have not love, I am nothing. ³ And though I bestow all my goods to feed the poor, and though I give my body to be burned, and have not love, it profits me nothing. *(NKJV)*

No matter how much or how little you have achieved in the Lord, you must measure yourself with the yardstick of God's love. These first three verses give us a unique perspective on Christian ministry:

- You can be the most gifted teacher and preacher on earth, able to speak profound truths in English and profound mysteries in tongues. But all those words are wasted if not spoken from a heart of love. You have *said* nothing.

- You can be the most charitable person on earth, working night and day like Mother Theresa. But if God's love is not your burning passion, your works won't do you any good. You *gain* nothing.

- You can be a miracle-worker for God, healing the sick, foretelling the future, and casting out demons. But if your miracles are not motivated by God's love, moving through your heart, you are just religious. You *are* nothing.

Years ago, I was looking for a new church fellowship and visited a church whose pastor was prominent on local radio and TV. The pastor was truly gifted, but I did not sense any love in the fellowship. It was not a complete ministry. I did not return there.

Let's continue with 1 Corinthians 13, verses 4–5:

[4] Love is patient, love is kind. It is not jealous, (love) is not pompous, it is not inflated, [5] it is not rude, it does not seek its own interests, it is not quick-tempered, it does not brood over injury. *(NAB)*

These two verses are a very succinct marriage manual. Your marriage will last a lifetime if both of you agree to:

- Be patient and kind toward your mate's shortcomings. This will help him/her be gracious toward yours.

- Understand that God gives different gifts to different people. Don't waste a millisecond envying your partner's gifts or boasting about your own. What do you have that you did not receive from Him?

- Behave appropriately when you are together. Since you are one flesh, your behavior will reflect either honor or dishonor on your mate.

- Remember that you have merged your lives, and have become as one body. If you seek your own agenda at the expense of your mate's, you are behaving as a cancer within the body. If your mate is behaving as a cancer, you should seek treatment. Consult your pastor.

- Be careful when you encounter areas of disagreement, which are actually opportunities for mutual growth. You will both grow in grace if you continually seek to strengthen the bond of love between you. Sincere apologies, accompanied by love in action, are coin of the realm.

- Resist the temptation to get "historical" during arguments. Forget the person that your mate used to be. Focus on the person that your mate is trying to become, and see what you can do to help him/her get there.

Re-read the above verses, substituting "Jesus" for "love," and remember that our primary aim is to follow Jesus and become more like Him.

Do this and live.

Verses 6 and 7 are general statements about how love looks in action:

[6] Rejoiceth not in iniquity, but rejoiceth in the truth; [7] Beareth all things, believeth all things, hopeth all things, endureth all things.

Now let's read verses 8–10 and try to maintain our sense of perspective:

[8] Love never fails. If there are prophecies, they will be brought to nothing; if tongues, they will cease; if knowledge, it will be brought to nothing. [9] For we know partially and we prophesy partially, [10] but when the perfect comes, the partial will pass away. *(NAB)*

When you read these verses in context, the meaning is clear. God expects our hearts to bear the fruit of His love, and He expects our actions to be motivated by His love.

As we have seen in the earlier verses, exercising love (a Fruit of the Holy Spirit) is more important than exercising prophecy or tongues (Gifts of the Holy Spirit). When we enter Eternal Life, we will retain our changed character but not necessarily our gifts. In Heaven, our knowledge will seem perfect compared to our present limited understanding.

Some mainline denominations and theology schools have devised a peculiar interpretation of this passage. They teach that "the perfect" in verse 10 is the Bible, and therefore the gifts of the Holy Spirit referred to in verses 8 and 9 (tongues and prophecy and knowledge) are no longer in operation and are no longer needed. Consider the implications of this interpretation:

- To believe this doctrine is to declare that any manifestation of these gifts since the second century A.D. must be from the devil and not the Holy Spirit.

- If the Holy Spirit really does give the gifts of tongues, prophecy and knowledge to believers today (Hint: He does.), then these teachers are attributing God's work to the devil. That could be interpreted as blasphemy against the Holy Spirit—the unpardonable sin, according to Jesus. Don't go there. It's OK to declare that the devil raises up lots of phony manifestations, because he does. I've encountered dozens of charismatic wolves in sheep's clothing, and so have you. But it's very risky to make a blanket statement that all manifestations of tongues and prophecy and healing are from the devil.

- To declare that we don't need the gifts of the Holy Spirit today is the height of arrogance. Human nature did not evolve to the next level with the publication of the King James Version or the invention of Bible Colleges.

- Since prophecy is telling forth the Word of God, and if the gift of prophecy stopped 1900 years ago, why are pastors from these denominations still ascending to the pulpit on Sundays? Every word spoken from the pulpit in Jesus' name should be God-breathed prophecy, holy to the Lord.

The very next verses prove that Paul did not refer to the Scriptures when he mentioned "the perfect" that was to come:

[11] When I was a child, I spoke as a child, I understood as a child, I thought as a child: but when I became a man, I put away childish things. [12] For now we see in a mirror, dimly; but then face-to-face. Now I know in part, but then I shall know just as I also am known. (NKJV)

If "the perfect" has already come, then verse 12 must already be true. So ask yourself, do all believers instantly get perfect wisdom and face-to-face understanding of God as soon as they start reading the Bible? Are these theology teachers perfect in their face-to-face experience of God? Do their faces shine like Moses' when they emerge from their prayer closets? I don't think so.

As usual, the plain meaning of Scripture makes more sense. Paul had been teaching about the gifts of the Spirit before he digressed into this chapter. He wanted to drill home the point that character change (brought about by love) has more value than operating in the gifts. Verse 13 reinforces that plain meaning:

[13] And now abide faith, hope, love, these three; but the greatest of these is love. (NKJV)

The obvious implication is that God wants to transform your life from the inside out, to equip you for ruling and reigning with Him during the Milennium. You must reflect His character before you can be trusted with a portion of His authority.

One other observation: We can have faith by ourselves, and feel a certain measure of love by ourselves, in isolation. But hope is a fragile, perishable commodity. We strengthen each other and renew each other in hope when we manifest the love of God toward our brothers and sisters in Christ.

That's why you should never miss an opportunity to make the love of God real for somebody. They might need a transfusion of hope (and the resulting boldness) more than you realize.

When I'm feeling down, don't bother telling me to be brave. Show me you care enough to spend time with me. Walk with me through the dark valley where my fears live. Let the love of God shine through your heart, to give me renewed hope and boldness.

Closing prayer: Lord, I'm so grateful that You love me so perfectly. Your love gives me the courage to go forward, through the dark valleys ahead. Let Your love transform my heart, that I may be a light shining in the dark valley, giving hope to my brothers and sisters in Christ. Amen.

Chapter 15

Blessings

Great blessings come out of great distress

"How long wilt Thou forget me, O LORD? For ever? How long wilt Thou hide Thy face from me?" *Psalm 13:1*

Opening Prayer: Lord, I know what it feels like to feel alone and neglected by my friends. Please help me understand the blessings You plan to bring into my life as a direct result of my faith during this difficult time.

Sometimes we hurt so bad we can't see straight. Sure, we've learned about spiritual warfare and we know that even "good" people suffer. We've even learned about the power of brokenness, and how we need to be emptied of our "stuff" before we can be completely filled with God's power.

We know that, as head knowledge. But in crisis times, we're still tempted to begin a sentence with the Five Most Dangerous Words in the English language.

Five Deadly Words

In my experience, the Five Most Dangerous Words are: "How could a loving God . . . ?

Starting a sentence with those five words is dangerous. They imply that you have more wisdom and knowledge than the God who created you. Fortunately, the Bible can teach us a healthier response to the difficulties of life.

Psalm 4, verse 1 gives us an important clue:

> [1] Hear me when I call, O God of my righteousness: **thou hast enlarged me** when I was in distress; have mercy upon me, and hear my prayer.

Some newer translations say, "You have relieved me . . ." instead of "Thou hast enlarged me" as the King James Version says. But the KJV is exactly right. The Hebrew word is *rachab*, which means to enlarge or to make wide.

There is an important lesson in this verse. When distress hits, my normal tendency is to pray for God to shrink the problem. However, God's preferred way of problem solving is *giving me more capacity* to deal with the problem.

But why does God let distressing things happen to us?

You might have trouble receiving this, but He allows distress because it's *good* for us.

Serious body builders get the most spectacular results by working specific muscle groups to the point of breakdown. Likewise, our spiritual "muscles" are strongest when God allows us to come to the end of our fleshly strength and understanding, and exercise faith in God and His Word.

Over the years, I've discovered that God arranges events in a particular sequence:

- Some events happen to cause me **distress**.

- On a good day, I realize that this distress appears to contradict a specific promise of God. So I make a **faith** decision to praise God and trust Him to get me through the time of distress.

- As a result of the distress and my faith action, God **enlarges** me and gives me more capacity to cope with problems.

- God always gives me some type of **blessing** as a result of my faith action and enlargement.

This pattern always holds true. When I exercise faith in response to pain and distress, God is able to enlarge me, and His power is released to bring blessings.

Unfortunately, the opposite also holds true: When I complain in response to distress, I'm on my own. God has no obligation to do something nice for me just because I'm assertive about my "rights" as a Christian.

Let's look at several Scriptures that concern our response to stress, starting at Psalm 18, verses 32–36:

> [32] It is God that girdeth me with strength, and maketh my way perfect. [33] He maketh my feet like hinds' feet, and setteth me upon my high places. [34] He teacheth my hands to war, so that a bow of steel is broken by mine arms. [35] Thou hast also given me the shield of thy salvation: and thy right hand hath holden me up, and thy gentleness hath made me great. [36] Thou hast enlarged my steps under me, that my feet did not slip.

Notice the flavor of these verses. This doesn't sound much like the peaceful pastures of Psalm 23. This sounds more like a soldier preparing to conduct guerilla warfare in some rocky hills. It's tough stuff, and not very politically correct. But this is what real life feels like.

Note especially verse 36: "Thou hast enlarged my steps under me . . ." Friends, this is not cute poetry. This is an important clue. Most of the time when hard times hit, we don't know which way to go. None of the choices seem very good. So what should we do? How do we get out of this mess?

God's answer is to *enlarge* the right way, to help us get to where we need to go.

Now let's read Psalm 119, verses 25–28:

> [25] My soul cleaveth unto the dust: quicken Thou me according to Thy word. [26] I have declared my ways, and Thou heardest me: teach me Thy statutes. [27] Make me to understand the way of Thy precepts: so shall I talk of Thy wondrous works. [28] My soul melteth for heaviness: strengthen Thou me according unto Thy word.

The plain truth is that life really does feel like this much of the time. But notice verse 28: the writer's response is to ask God to give him more strength—the enlarging that we've talked about.

Now let's read verses 29–32:

> [29] Remove from me the way of lying: and grant me Thy law graciously. [30] I have chosen the way of truth: Thy judgments have I laid before me. [31] I have stuck unto Thy testimonies: O LORD, put me not to shame. [32] I will run the way of Thy commandments, when Thou shalt enlarge my heart.

This passage tells us some important truths. When the poopy times hit, we have to make a choice. Do we choose to believe the lie that God is not in control or not loving? Or will we choose to believe that God is loving and gracious?

Note what David says here: "I have *chosen* the way of truth . . ." and "I have *stuck* to Thy testimonies . . ." and "I will *run* the way of Thy commandments . . ."—When? When Thou shalt *enlarge* my heart.

Remember the cycle: Distress, Faith Action, Enlargement, and Blessing.

For further emphasis, let's look at verses 67 and 71:

> [67] Before I was afflicted I went astray: but now have I kept Thy word. [71] It is good for me that I have been afflicted; that I might learn Thy statutes.

Verse 67 states the obvious—that our fleshly natures are weak and prone to stray from God's path. Therefore, verse 71 makes it clear that a Loving God does allow us to endure suffering, whether we approve or not.

Now let's turn to the New Testament, the Book of Hebrews, chapter 11, verses 1–3:

> [1] Now faith is the substance of things hoped for, the evidence of things not seen. [2] For by it the elders obtained a good report. [3] Through faith we understand that the worlds were framed by the word of God, so that things which are seen were not made of things which do appear.

The key here is that faith is the response that God wants from us when bad times hit. And it's only faith if we believe in God's promise when His answer isn't in view. Faith gives substance to what we hope for, and it is evidence of things not seen.

Now verses 4–6:

> ⁴ By faith Abel offered unto God a more excellent sacrifice than Cain, by which he obtained witness that he was righteous, God testifying of his gifts: and by it he being dead yet speaketh. ⁵ By faith Enoch was translated that he should not see death; and was not found, because God had translated him: for before his translation he had this testimony, that he pleased God. ⁶ But without faith it is impossible to please Him: for he that cometh to God must believe that He is, and that He is a rewarder of them that diligently seek Him.

At first, everything about being a Christian required some type of faith action:

- It took faith to keep dragging myself to church services (because so many of the first churches I visited did not show any signs of intelligent life much less any life in the Holy Spirit).

- It took faith to begin reading the bible, which sounded boring and stuffy at first.

- It took faith to begin tithing.

- It took great faith to begin sharing my faith, because I was sure of being rejected.

- It took faith to pray longer than three minutes at a time.

- It took faith to let go of my worldly party habits.

- It took faith to get involved in Christian fellowship, because the "born-again" folks looked boring and weird.

Today, I can cruise through these actions without exercising any faith whatever. And so can you, my friend. We can go along for days and weeks at a time in our religious groove and not commit any overt sin. But we haven't exercised any faith, either, have we?

The scary part is that when you and I cruise through a faithless day, we are probably unaware of it. But God knows.

The sad part is that we only get a few years down here to store up the rewards of faith, and a faithless day is a complete waste of time.

Sadder still, many of us in ministry situations will have failed to feed our sheep that day. We will work hard, do our very best, come home exhausted and feel burned out with the ministry work. All for naught, if not in faith.

Now let's jump farther down in Hebrews 11, to verses 32–39:

> [32] And what shall I more say? for the time would fail me to tell of Gideon, and of Barak, and of Samson, and of Jephtha; of David also, and Samuel, and of the prophets: [33] Who through faith subdued kingdoms, wrought righteousness, obtained promises, stopped the mouths of lions, [34] Quenched the violence of fire, escaped the edge of the sword, out of weakness were made strong, waxed valiant in fight, turned to flight the armies of the aliens. [35] Women received their dead raised to life again: and others were tortured, not accepting deliverance; that they might obtain a better resurrection: [36] And others had trial of cruel mockings and scourgings, yea, moreover of bonds and imprisonment: [37] They were stoned, they were sawn asunder, were tempted, were slain with the sword: they wandered about in sheepskins and goatskins; being destitute, afflicted, tormented; [38] (Of whom the world was not worthy:) they wandered in deserts, and in mountains, and in dens and caves of the earth. [39] And these all, having obtained a good report through faith, received not the promise.

Look at verse 34. Have any of us been chased by people wielding swords or pistols this week? Have we suffered the torture that the Romans used to inflict on Christians? Maybe a few of you, but most of us have had an easier time of it this week.

Now let's read Hebrews 12, verses 1–2:

> [1] Wherefore seeing we also are compassed about with so great a cloud of witnesses, let us lay aside every weight, and the sin which doth so easily beset us, and let us run with patience the race that is set before us, [2] Looking unto Jesus the author and finisher of our faith; who for the joy that was set before him endured the cross, despising the shame, and is set down at the right hand of the throne of God.

The "cloud of witnesses" is a reference to the saints we read about in the Bible, plus those we know who have walked the road of faith ahead of us. These witnesses tell us, "You can make it, my friend!"

You *can* make it, by faith

In response to this exhortation, let's heed the advice of verse one, and set aside the weaknesses of the flesh which try to hold us back. Moving forward in faith requires us to say "No!" to the devil and our flesh. Moving forward in faith requires us to say "Yes!" to God and the promises of Scripture.

That's really hard sometimes. But look at Hebrews 12, verses 3–4:

> ³ For consider Him that endured such contradiction of sinners against Himself, lest ye be wearied and faint in your minds. ⁴ Ye have not yet resisted unto blood, striving against sin.

It's only human to be weary and faint-hearted when we're going through tough times. So the writer says, "Consider Jesus. Look unto Him, and think what He did for you and for me."

Now let's read Hebrews 12, verses 5–8:

> ⁵ And ye have forgotten the exhortation which speaketh unto you as unto children, My son, despise not thou the chastening of the Lord, nor faint when thou art rebuked of Him: ⁶ For whom the Lord loveth he chasteneth, and scourgeth every son whom He receiveth. ⁷ If ye endure chastening, God dealeth with you as with sons; for what son is he whom the father chasteneth not? ⁸ But if ye be without chastisement, whereof all are partakers, then are ye bastards, and not sons.

Pay close attention to verse 7, saying that God wants to deal with you as *sons*. Sons were considered a sign of favor from the Lord, and ranked ahead of daughters in terms of power and inheritance. Therefore this verse is saying that Christian women who endure God's chastening in faith will receive eternal favor and inheritance second to none. Think about it.

Now verses 9–11:

> ⁹ Furthermore we have had fathers of our flesh which corrected us, and we gave them reverence: shall we not much rather be in subjection unto the Father of spirits, and live? ¹⁰ For they verily for a few days chastened us after their own pleasure; but He for our profit, that we might be partakers of His holiness. ¹¹ Now no chastening for the present seemeth to be joyous, but grievous: nevertheless afterward it

yieldeth the peaceable fruit of righteousness unto them which are exercised thereby.

Verse 11 appears to state the obvious, since everybody knows that chastening is grievous. But when we're hurting, it's too easy to forget that the chastening (or affliction or distress or whatever you call it) is the essential first step in God's path to blessing for us. Distress, followed by our faith, inevitably leads to enlargement and blessing.

Let's read verses 12–15:

[12] Wherefore lift up the hands which hang down, and the feeble knees; [13] And make straight paths for your feet, lest that which is lame be turned out of the way; but let it rather be healed. [14] Follow peace with all men, and holiness, without which no man shall see the Lord: [15] Looking diligently lest any man fail of the grace of God; lest any root of bitterness springing up trouble you, and thereby many be defiled;

Verse 15 warns us against those Five Dangerous Words we talked about. When bad times hit, we can say those Five Dangerous Words and indulge in that root of bitterness. Or we can act in faith, trusting in the faithfulness and grace of God.

Praise: A Powerful Response

So what should we do to demonstrate faith in response to distress? Praising God is an excellent way to start. Several helpful things happen when you praise God in the midst of crummy circumstances:

- When you praise God sincerely during hardship, you exercise faith in God's promises, and thereby gain eternal rewards.

- When you praise God aloud during hardship, you speak words of faith to your own soul. This will help calm your involuntary fears.

- When you praise God during hardship, you shatter the devil's influence in the situation. Satan might have been involved in bringing the hardship upon you, but it drives him crazy when you give God the glory anyway. Your faith and your persistent praise will drive the devil right out of the room. Conversely, when you complain and blame God, you give Satan handles by which he can steer you around like a scooter.

- Persistently praising God through hardship builds endurance, joy and faithfulness in your character—fruit of the Holy Spirit and evidence of God's power at work in your life. This will be a powerful testimony to your friends and family that Jesus Christ is the same yesterday, today and forever. When God brings the enlargement and the blessing (and He certainly will), your friends and family will have proof that God's promises in Scripture are true.

Let's close by repeating Psalm 119, verses 30–32:

[30] I have chosen the way of truth: Thy judgments have I laid before me. [31] I have stuck unto Thy testimonies: O LORD, put me not to shame. [32] I will run the way of Thy commandments, when Thou shalt enlarge my heart.

Friends, a lot of us have experienced distress and pain this past couple of weeks. Let me encourage you to spend extra time waiting on the Lord this week. Delight yourself in Him. Listen for His voice. Spend extra time praising Him out loud tonight and tomorrow morning and tomorrow night. Then wait quietly before Him, like a child in a parent's lap.

Closing Prayer: Lord, I repent of all the religious days when I walked in my own strength and complained about my problems. Thank you for dealing with me as Your son. I praise You for Your love and grace towards me. Enlarge me and let me shine as a testimony to Your faithfulness, I pray. Amen.

Chapter 16

Backsliding

Does Jesus really care?

[2] I know your works and your labor and your patience . . . and for My name's sake you have labored and have not fainted. [4] But I have this against you: that you have left your first love. [5] Therefore remember from where you have fallen, and repent, and do the first works, or else I will come to you quickly and will remove your lampstand out of its place unless you repent. *Revelation 2:2–5 (MKJV)*

Opening Prayer: Lord, how did I ever get to this point? When did my love for you begin cooling off? When did I start letting other treasures ensnare my heart? Show me how to return to that place of my first love, I pray.

*H*uman love is really peculiar. We meet a special person and our lives are changed. The sky is bluer and the clouds are whiter. We hear angels singing when we're with our loved one. Time flies by too quickly. We cry when we must be apart for more than a few hours. Surely this person is a gift from God, and we pledge undying love at the altar of matrimony.

Then real life steps in. We start finding fault. Our spouse begins looking familiar and ordinary, rather than perfect and wonderful. Our passion cools. Unless we wake up and invest some energy in the relationship, it will die.

Many times, our relationship with Jesus is exactly like that. When I first discovered the truth of the Gospel, that Jesus loved me enough to die for me, to pay the price for my redemption, my joy and love for Him knew no bounds. For nearly a year, I just couldn't get enough of the Bible and church services. I wanted to tell every person I met about Jesus.

But eventually my fervor began to cool. My faith felt pretty ordinary, and I wasn't quite as excited about the Lord. Then one of the pastors enlightened me about prayer and my love for Jesus was renewed wonderfully. For awhile.

Looking back over the past 20 years, I can see how my love for God has been inconsistent. At times my heart burns with love for Him. At other times, I've been lukewarm and didn't realize it.

Cooling slowly

When I'm in the process of backsliding, I'm the last one to know it. Backsliding is very comfortable. I'm still pointing toward God—at first. Then my eyes and my heart are distracted and drawn away to other treasures. When I finally wake up to my condition, I've wandered off the trail. My fervent love for the Lord has cooled, and I realize that I've wasted time and opportunities.

Jesus gives a stern warning about this cooling-off process in Revelation 3, verses 15–18:

> [15] I know your works, that you are neither cold nor hot. I would that you were cold or hot. [16] So because you are lukewarm, and neither cold nor hot, I will vomit you out of My mouth. [17] Because you say, I am rich and increased with goods and have need of nothing, and do not know that you are wretched and miserable and poor and blind and naked, [18] I counsel you to buy from Me gold purified by fire, so that you may be rich; and white clothing, so that you may be clothed, and *so that* the shame of your nakedness does not appear. And anoint your eyes with eye salve, so that you may see. *(MKJV)*

Remember that Jesus was talking to Christians, not heathen folks. His listeners were still going to church, still putting money into the offering, still reading their Bibles. They were still involved in ministry. But they had lost the passion that once burned in their hearts.

This is a truly frightening place to be. When we cool off, we stop exercising faith. Our feet still walk inside the church building, and our mouths still say the words, but our hearts aren't in it. We're just being religious. Our faith has become head knowledge, lifeless and powerless. Like the seed that falls among thorns, our hearts have become choked by the cares of this life, and our lives are unfruitful. We should be salt and light. Instead, we're tasteless and dim.

Fortunately, Jesus gives us a simple solution in verses 19 and 20:

> [19] As many as I love, I rebuke and chasten; therefore be zealous and repent. [20] Behold, I stand at the door and knock. If anyone hears My voice and opens the door, I will come in to him and will dine with him and he with Me. (*MKJV*)

Wake up, receive the rebuke of our Lord and Savior, and realize that He still loves you. Then be zealous and repent. The Holy Spirit will rekindle the fire in your heart if you give Him permission.

You might have heard pastors using verse 20 to invite non-believers to come forward, to give their lives to Jesus for the first time. But in context, you realize that it's for *you*—the backsliding believer. When you have backslid long enough, you have locked Jesus outside your heart.

Jesus still loves you and still wants to have fellowship with you. But the door has only one handle—on the inside. You must repent of your lukewarmness, or you might find yourself outside the door of Heaven with all the other unbelievers.

Is it ever too late?

At some point, the backsliding stops. The former believer just stops caring about Jesus. Never mind the excuses and the "reasons." The former believer is now a hardened sinner, vaccinated by religion and seemingly immune to the Gospel of grace.

Don't deceive yourself with the slogan "Once saved, always saved." That's a doctrine of man. Jesus never said that, nor did any of the Apostles. In Luke 9 we read:

> [62] And Jesus said to him, No one, having put his hand to the plow and looking back, is fit for the kingdom of God.

Jesus said, "Be zealous and repent." Jesus says to get over being luke-warm or risk being vomited out of His mouth.

In deep water

Unfortunately, most folks in this position feel trapped. Maybe they've become slaves to a drug or a bottle. Maybe they've become tangled in a bad relationship or hooked on pornography or sexual perversion.

The trapped person wonders, "Why should I care? Does anybody care? Does even God care about me anymore? Am I going to die in this condition?"

Backwards as it may seem, God still cares. God is still concerned about you. The Holy Spirit still has the life-changing power to set you free from bondage, if you are willing. Are you willing to be set free? As long as you still have breath, you can use it to call out for mercy and forgiveness.

In Mark's gospel, chapter 4, Jesus' disciples were so frightened that they cried out:

[38] "Master, carest thou not that we perish?"

The basic story is probably familiar to you. Jesus and His disciples had entered a boat to cross the Sea of Galilee. After Jesus fell asleep, a ferocious storm arose. This was not a gentle Spring rain. This storm was bad enough to make even the disciples—experienced sailors—fear for their lives.

So what did Jesus do about it? Let's see the next verse:
[39] And He arose, and rebuked the wind, and said unto the sea, "Peace, be still." And the wind ceased, and there was a great calm.

A great calm: I like the sound of that. In fact, I could use more of that calm stuff. What about you?

Don't kid yourself that this was a special case. Obviously Jesus was willing to save His disciples, but we know from other passages that He cares passionately for every single lost sheep.

How can I *know* He cares about *me*?

Good question. People have been asking that for more than 1900 years now. In fact, Paul addressed this issue in his letter to the Hebrews, chapter 4:

[15] For we have not an high priest which cannot be touched with the feeling of our infirmities; but was in all points tempted like as we are, yet without sin. [16] Let us therefore come boldly unto the throne of grace, that we may obtain mercy, and find grace to help in time of need.

Our Lord Jesus walked the earth in human flesh. He personally experienced hunger, thirst, pain and great weariness. He remembers how it feels to be betrayed by "friends." He remembers the pain and shame of the brutal Roman crucifixion, which He willingly endured—for you. In return, we must remember that His blessings come to us on the basis of grace—gifts we did not earn.

At times, I've heard people say, "If God is so merciful and loving, why am I hurting so bad? If you had my problems, you'd sing a different song!"

Not necessarily. My friend Marvin had quite extensive "challenges" (to use a modern euphemism), and still loved to praise the Lord. Marvin was blind, like many of his fellow students in the Special Education class I taught years ago. Marvin played the piano and led the singing for this amazing group of dedicated saints.

Each Sunday, Marvin would sing a solo. His favorite (and mine) was an old hymn written by Frank Graeff and J. Lincoln Hall titled "Does Jesus Care?" The first verse and chorus are:

> Does Jesus care when my heart is pained
> Too deeply for mirth and song,
> As the burdens press, and the cares distress,
> And the way grows weary and long?
> O yes, He cares. I know He cares!
> His heart is touched with my grief.
> When the days are weary, the long nights dreary,
> I know my Savior cares.

Can you sense the ring of truth in these words? We know that when Jesus walked this earth 2000 years ago, His heart was frequently touched by the grief and pain of those around Him. We frequently read that Jesus was moved with compassion.

Marvin usually concluded with the second verse and the chorus:

> Does Jesus care when my way is dark
> With a nameless dread and fear?

As the daylight fades into deep night shades,
Does He care enough to be near?
O yes, He cares. I know He cares!
His heart is touched with my grief.
When the days are weary, the long nights dreary,
I know my Savior cares.

This second verse would get me, as I watched this wonderful saint play and sing. This man had been able to see as a child, before a disease took away his vision. In his life, the daylight truly had faded into deep night shades. And the daylight never came back. But Marvin truly experienced the nearness of the Lord through all those dark years.

Touched by the experience, I looked for and found the song in an old Baptist hymnal. And discovered two additional verses. The third verse says:

Does Jesus care when I've tried and failed
To resist some temptation strong;
When for my deep grief I find no relief,
Tho my tears flow all the night long?
O yes, He cares. I know He cares!
His heart is touched with my grief.
When the days are weary, the long nights dreary,
I know my Savior cares.

Have I failed to resist? Yeah. Over the past 50 years, I've fallen for some really stupid and ordinary temptations, and felt absolutely shattered afterwards. How could I be so foolish? And how could a holy God ever forgive me?

The answer is that God's forgiveness is everywhere in Scripture. One of the most extreme examples is that of Simon Peter, who vehemently denied that he even knew Jesus. Yet Jesus personally sought Peter after His resurrection—not to condemn Peter but to offer forgiveness and restoration. Remarkable.

The fourth verse didn't become real for me until a couple of years later, when my wife left me:

Does Jesus care when I've said goodbye
To the dearest on earth to me;
And my sad heart aches till it nearly breaks,
Is it aught to Him? Does He see?

That was one of the darkest times of my life. Each day I would cry out to the Lord, seeking peace and comfort—that perfect peace promised in Scripture and available nowhere else in the universe. Each day, the Lord heard my cry and gave me peace, comfort and true joy. Despite the dreary circumstances and my unworthiness, the Lord was faithful to His promises. Somehow, I was able to sing:

> O yes, He cares. I know He cares!
> His heart is touched with my grief.
> When the days are weary, the long nights dreary,
> I know my Savior cares.

My friend, Jesus does care about you. Wherever you are in your walk, and no matter how badly you have fallen, Jesus knows where you are and waits to receive you to Himself. He can set you free, change your heart and restore your joy. Turn back to Him with all your heart, and learn the truth of Revelation 3:20 again:

> [20] Behold, I stand at the door and knock. If anyone hears My voice and opens the door, I will come in to him and will dine with him and he with Me.

Closing prayer: Father, I have sinned and left my first love. But I know—by faith—that Your promises are true and trustworthy. Guide me by Your Holy Spirit, to return to the path of joy and fellowship with Jesus, I pray. Amen.

Chapter 17

Joy in Worship

The ultimate test of sincerity

⁶ Oh come, let us worship and bow down; let us kneel before Jehovah our maker.
Psalm 95:6 (MKJV)

Opening Prayer: Heavenly Father, You created everything. You have all power and glory. You have perfect self-esteem. What types of worship do You want from me and why? Help me understand Your plan, I pray. Amen.

Today's vocabulary word is "worship." To quote from Webster's Dictionary, the word comes from "Middle English worshipe worthiness, respect, reverence paid to a divine being, from Old English weorthscipe worthiness, respect; derived from weorth worthy, worth + -scipe —ship."

Worship expresses how we value God. But does our worship measure up to the Bible's patterns? Do you and I really worship God with all of our hearts?

The Gate of Worship

Most of the time, we don't feel like worshipping God, because He seems so far away. We can't see Him or hear Him. It feels like God is on the other side of a solid wall.

Fortunately, the Lord has provided a gate to enable us to enter in to His presence and worship Him. This gate is open 24 hours per day, and admission is almost free. There is a tiny price to pay for admission, as we see in Psalm 100:

> [4] Enter into His gates with thanksgiving, and into His courts with praise. Be thankful to Him, and bless His name.

A thankful heart gets you inside the gate. Lifting your voice in praise will bring you into His courtyard, to meet Him face to face.

God's eyes are not fooled by appearances. You can't fake gratitude. He isn't deceived when you sing a praise song from memory rather than your heart. He knows when your body is in church and your mind is on Venus or Mars.

When your heart is broken before Him, He knows. When your eyes are filled with tears of repentance, and you are conscious of how short you have fallen, He hears you. When you are truly broken-hearted before Him, He will lift you up, as we see in Psalm 34:

> [17] The righteous cry, and the LORD heareth, and delivereth them out of all their troubles. [18] The LORD *is* nigh unto them that are of a broken heart; and saveth such as be of a contrite spirit.

Backwards as it sounds, brokenness and praise are essential to worship. If you truly understand this concept, it will change your life forever.

Just remember that the Christian life is a battle zone. The greatest warfare takes place around worship, especially our morning devotional prayer time.

Every morning, the Holy Spirit calls us to enter into His presence with thanksgiving and praise. And every morning, the powers of darkness encourage our sleepy flesh to resist the Lord's invitation.

Most mornings, it's a real step of faith to push our tired bodies to the prayer closet. It's crucial that we trust God and consciously prepare for the battles that we will face each day. If we leave our houses without our armor, we are vulnerable to ambush. Our families will be at risk.

Backwards as it sounds, this real-looking world around us is not our permanent home. It's a battle zone, and we're called to stand—in His strength and grace—until the Lord returns to bring us home. Paul writes about his in his letter to the Hebrews, chapter 13:

> [14] For here we have no continuing city, but we seek one to come. [15] By Him, then, let us offer the sacrifice of praise to God continually, that is, *the* fruit of our lips, confessing His name. *(MKJV)*

Before we leave the shelter of our homes, we must strengthen our hearts in preparation for the rest of the day—especially if the day includes worship in a public church service or home fellowship group.

"Worship" Services

A broken, grateful heart is essential to personal worship. In public church services, however, displays of emotion can be a problem for two reasons:

- Emotional displays can be fleshly or faked. The genuine brokenness of revival cannot be sustained for long. It will inevitably dissipate or be displaced by fleshly or ritualistic behavior.

- If a non-believer visits a church service and finds himself surrounded by a thousand people sobbing for no apparent reason, he or she will make a quick exit. It's hard for a stranger to discern between fake and genuine tears of joy and repentance.

The key is that we believers must prepare our hearts early every morning. We must enter into God's holy presence with thanksgiving and praise every morning, long before we enter the church building. We must continue in that attitude of praise all day as part of the whole armor (panoply) of God, as we saw in Ephesians 6:

> [18] Praying always with all prayer and supplication in the Spirit, and watching thereunto with all perseverance and supplication for all saints.

Notice the second part of verse 18. We must extend the realm of our prayer to include our brothers and sisters in Christ. This includes a time of dedicated prayer before every church service. Believers must pray for:

- An anointing on the teaching pastor, that he may proclaim God's Word in the power of the Holy Spirit.

- An anointing on all the other pastors and workers, as they minister to the flock of God.

- An anointing on ourselves, that our words may build up our brothers and sisters in Christ, and touch the hearts of unbelieving visitors.

- An anointing upon every believer in the building, that he or she may reflect the love of Jesus Christ to those who don't yet know Him.

- A spiritual shield around the church grounds, that the religious spirits and powers of darkness may be unable to operate there.

Our prayers must continue during the church service or home fellowship group. Many of the brothers and sisters around you are hurting, with problems they might not tell you about. Ask the Lord to help you see your neighbors as He sees them, and to love them as He loves them.

When the service is finished, let the Holy Spirit lead you in conversation with your neighbors. Listen for opportunities to encourage or strengthen, and resist the temptation to feel smug or superior. Pride will immediately disqualify you from ministry. You cannot make the love of Jesus real for anyone that you feel superior to.

So far, we have only touched on a few basic principles. Now let's look to Psalm 95 for deeper insights into worship.

Worship Lesson

The first verse of Psalm 95 sounds very peculiar to us Americans:

[1] Oh come, let us sing unto the LORD: let us make a joyful noise to the rock of our salvation.

The singing part sounds reasonable, but what about the shouting? These days, it's not considered polite to shout about anything except a sporting event or a rock concert.

So let's turn the thought around. People shout at football games because they're excited and emotionally involved. Shouldn't Christians be excited and emotionally involved with their relationship to God? Certainly!

Christians should be the most-animated and most-excited people on the planet. Just in the pages of this book we've already discovered plenty to shout about:

- God loves us, despite our failings.

- God's only Son, Jesus, loved us enough to suffer a horrible death to pay the penalty of our sins.

- We can receive eternal life as a free gift, through faith in Jesus.

- Jesus, our Good Shepherd, cares for us in good times and bad.

- Jesus is the Rock of our salvation; we can run to Him and be safe.

- The Holy Spirit comforts us with gifts of healings and words of prophecy.

- The Holy Spirit works on yielded hearts, bringing miraculous character change in us, including durable joy.

Now let's consider the military implications of Psalm 95, verse one. The second part of verse one says: Let us shout joyfully to the Rock of our salvation.

The very word "salvation" implies that we need to be saved from something dangerous. In both the Hebrew and Greek, "salvation" includes deliverance from all types of evil: physical, spiritual and emotional. Jehovah God is our Rock—our immovable fortress, our place of refuge above the flood waters and out of our enemy's reach.

We cannot take God's protection for granted. We must maintain our sense of gratitude, as we see in verse 2:

[2] Let us come before His presence with thanksgiving, and make a joyful noise unto Him with psalms.

If we really understand what God has provided for us, we will be thankful and joyful. His love for us is amazing, in view of verses 3–5:

[3] For Jehovah is a great God, and a great King above all gods. [4] In His hand are the deep places of the earth; the strength of the hills is also His. [5] The sea is His, and He made it, and His hands formed the dry land. (MKJV)

We must never become casual in our prayers to God. He has all power and authority in His hands. No man or beast can draw breath without His permission. Even our problems are part of His plan, as He restrains the powers of darkness from completely destroying us.

Verse 6 tells us the appropriate response to encountering Jehovah God:

> [6] O come, let us worship and bow down: let us kneel before the LORD our maker.

It isn't easy for Americans to physically bow to anybody. But verse 6 above uses three Hebrew action verbs to reinforce the concept:

- *Worship* translates *shachah,* to stoop or fall flat on your face. This is similar in meaning to the most-common Greek word for worship, *proskuneo,* to crouch or bow or prostrate oneself in homage, implying a vast difference in power and status.
- *Bow down* translates *kara,* to bend the knee.
- *Kneel* translates *barak,* to kneel down on both knees and prostrate yourself.

Equals do not bow like this to each other. God is not just an evolved human being. Humans are not gods in training. He is God, and we are not. We must swallow our pride and worship Him.

Pride has no place in worship. We created nothing. We deserve nothing. We have no rights. We have nothing of value to God except our love and trust. God will not bow Himself to you.

The last five verses help to put His power and authority in context:

> [7] For He is our God; and we are the people of His pasture, and the sheep of His hand. To day if ye will hear His voice, [8] Harden not your heart, as in the provocation, and as in the day of temptation in the wilderness: [9] When your fathers tempted Me, proved Me, and saw My work. [10] For forty years I was grieved with this generation, and said, It is a people who go astray in their hearts, and they have not known My ways; [11] to whom I swore in My wrath that they should not enter into My rest. (*MKJV*)

As verse 7 points out, God leads us like a patient shepherd. But we must love and obey our Shepherd. Some of the Israelites exhausted God's patience and never entered the Promised Land. We must learn from their mistakes.

Heart worship is the necessary first step. When our hearts are right, they will overflow with thankfulness. We sense a need to worship God with more than just our words. Someday we must learn to open our wallets as well as our mouths.

Worship in Giving

Giving to God really sounds backwards to me. After all, He created everything and has the power to create more of anything. It seems even crazier to give to God through churches. Many of them appear big and prosperous already, without any help from us.

So why does God devote so many pages in the Bible to the offerings He wants us to give Him?

The difficult truth is that you and I *need* to give regularly, in order to be healthy. Stranger yet, we get healthier and more prosperous when we learn to give generously, according to the patterns in the Bible.

The Checkbook Offering

For some reason, many American Christians feel intimidated by the thought of giving a tithe, a tenth of one's income, to the Church. It seems like a huge sacrifice to some of us.

Actually, the tithe is not prominently discussed in the Old Testament, mentioned fewer than a dozen times in the Law. Furthermore, the tithe was just the starting point. Israelites were expected to give a tithe as a minimum, and then give a variety of other offerings.

The book of Leviticus is primarily about offerings, but tithes aren't mentioned until the last paragraph of the last chapter. Leviticus 27 tells us:

> [30] "All the tithe of the land, whether of the seed of the land or of the fruit of the trees, is the LORD's; it is holy to the LORD. [31] "If a man wishes to redeem any of his tithe, he shall add a fifth to it. [32] "And all the tithe of herds and flocks, every tenth animal of all that pass under the herdsman's staff, shall be holy to the LORD. [33] "A man shall not inquire whether it is good or bad, neither shall he exchange it; and if he exchanges it, then both it and that for which it is exchanged shall be holy; it shall not be redeemed." (*RSV*)

In one respect, the tithe was the foundation for giving. Giving the tithe was a constant reminder that all we have comes from Him, and that we trust Him to meet our needs. But God didn't spend much time describing tithes.

By comparison, God spent more time telling Moses about all the other types of offerings He wanted. The peculiar aspect of the Old Testament offerings is that each presents a different picture of Jesus, depicting His sacrificial death on the cross and other aspects of His relationship with His Father. In addition, each has a specific relevance to our walk with the Lord.

For your homework, spend a couple of evenings reading through and taking notes on the book of Leviticus. Write down each type of offering, its purpose, and its relevance to your walk with the Lord.

Pay particular attention to the *burnt offerings*, sometimes called the *sweet savor* offerings. Unlike other offerings, these were entirely consumed on the altar. No part was held back by the priests as their portion or returned to the giver like a fellowship offering. The entire thing was consumed before the Lord.

These burnt offerings are God's favorites. A modern equivalent might be putting cash in the offering plate and not asking for a receipt for your tax-deductible donation. Another might be a truly anonymous gift to a needy family in your community.

The burnt offering is the exact opposite of a designated offering, where a wealthy donor contributes a large sum toward construction of a new building or establishing scholarships in his or her name. Just remember what Jesus said about giving in Matthew 6:

> [1] When you do good deeds, don't try to show off. If you do, you won't get a reward from your Father in Heaven. [2] When you give to the poor, don't blow a loud horn. That's what show-offs do in the meeting places and on the street corners, because they are always looking for praise. I can assure you that they already have their reward. [3] When you give to the poor, don't let anyone know about it. [4] Then your gift will be given in secret. Your Father knows what is done in secret, and He will reward you. (*CEV*)

We will talk more about rewards in the next chapter, "Bema Rewards."

Healthy vs. Dangerous Worship

We must never allow worship to become a comfortable tradition. Each day, we must seek God afresh, like the Israelites harvesting manna each morning. Yesterday's thanksgiving won't help us find the gate today. We must encounter our Lord as our first priority every morning, and maintain the attitude of worship throughout the day.

The most dangerous form of worship is that which doesn't require any effort or faith on your part. If you've come to enjoy church services because of the singing and the chance to chat with your friends, be careful. Remember the words of Hebrews 11:

> [6] But without faith *it is* impossible to please *Him*, for he who comes to God must believe that He is and *that* He is a rewarder of those who diligently seek Him. *(MKJV)*

Another dangerous practice is giving God less than your best. Hear the words of the prophet Malachi:

> [1:6] A son honors his father, and a servant his master. If then I *am* a father, where is My honor? And if I *am* a master, where is My fear? says Jehovah of Hosts to you, O priests who despise My name. And you say, In what way have we despised Your name? [7] You offer defiled bread upon My altar; and you say, In what way have we defiled You? In your saying, The table of Jehovah, it *is* a thing to be despised. [8] And if you offer the blind for sacrifice, *is it* not evil? And if you offer the lame and the sick, *is it* not evil? Bring it now to your governor. Will he accept you, or lift up your face, says Jehovah of Hosts? *(MKJV)*

These days, we don't bring blind or lame sheep to church. But we might donate a worn-out sofa or refrigerator to the church. Such a donation might be helpful to a needy family if your church has this type of ministry. But don't confuse this donation with an offering to the Lord. God deserves your best, not your trash.

Malachi had more to say about offerings in chapter 3:

> [8] Will a man rob God? Yet you have robbed Me. But you say, In what have we robbed You? In the tithe and the offering! [9] You *are* cursed with a curse; for you *are* robbing Me, the nation, all of it. [10] Bring all the tithe into the storehouse, so that there may be food in My house. **And test Me now with this, says Jehovah of Hosts**, to see if I will not

open the windows of Heaven for you, and pour out a blessing for you, until *there is* not enough *room*. [11] And I will rebuke your devourer, and he shall not decay the fruit of your ground against you; nor shall your vine miscarry against you in the field, says Jehovah of Hosts. *(MKJV)*

God doesn't say "test Me" very often, so pay attention. God is not interested in what percentage of your income you give Him. God is interested in your heart attitude.

Do you trust God to provide all your needs? Do you trust God to protect your assets and your family through difficult times? If you love and trust God, your giving will reflect it. And He will multiply your joy and blessings beyond measure.

Worship in Giving Your Time

In Leviticus 23 God describes different feast days that are connected to different types of offerings. The first comes as a surprise to us:

[1] And the LORD spake unto Moses, saying, [2] "Speak unto the children of Israel, and say unto them *concerning* the feasts of the LORD, which ye shall proclaim *to be* holy convocations, *even* these *are* my feasts. [3] "Six days shall work be done: but the seventh day *is* the Sabbath of rest, an holy convocation; ye shall do no work *therein*: it *is* the Sabbath of the LORD in all your dwellings."

We don't normally expect to see the Sabbath day included in a list of religious holidays, but it leads the parade. Actually the Sabbath day is a profound offering—setting aside one day per week as holy to the Lord. In addition to money, we should give our time and attention to the Lord.

Those of you who own farms or small retail businesses understand the issue. It's hard to take a Sabbath rest from the demands of the business. It takes real faith to dedicate one day per week to serving the Lord when there is always urgent work to do.

On the other hand, some of you city dwellers don't see the problem. You ask, "What's the big deal about taking a one-day break from the job? I get *two* days off every weekend!" True, most of us work five days (or less) per week. But do we really dedicate one of our two weekend days completely to serving the Lord?

Jesus gives us an interesting perspective in the gospel of Mark, chapter 2:

[27] And He said unto them, "The Sabbath was made for man, and not man for the Sabbath."

God did not ordain the Sabbath so we could act religious once per week. God ordained the Sabbath because we need the rest. Our minds and hearts and bodies can't run continuously like the planets in their orbits. We need periodic rest, because God designed us that way. We need to spend at least one day per week focused on Him and the Holy Scriptures.

Psalm 23 gives us another insight into proper use of the Sabbath:

[3] He restoreth my soul. He leadeth me in the paths of righteousness for His name's sake.

Like a carpenter restoring a worn cabinet or a mechanic restoring an older car, God can touch and mend a wounded soul. If we give the Sabbath day to God as a day to rest and abide in Him, we give Him permission to restore our battered hearts. As we meditate on God's Scripture and abide in Him, we can follow Jesus in the way of righteousness.

The Sabbath day of rest helps restore our souls. It encourages us to follow Jesus down the narrow path, following the clear tracks He and the disciples left for us in the Scriptures. Abiding in Jesus enables us to leave clear tracks for our family and friends to follow.

Whether you dedicate Saturday, Sunday or Wednesday to the Lord, resolve to make at least *one* day per week a holy offering of time to the Lord.

The Sabbath Year

God knows human nature pretty well. He knows we can get comfortable taking one day of rest per week. So He determined a different type of Sabbath to be a true test of character. In Leviticus 25 we read:

[1] And Jehovah spoke to Moses in Mount Sinai, saying, [2] Speak to the sons of Israel and say to them, When you come into the land which I give you, then shall the land keep a sabbath to Jehovah. [3] You shall sow your field six years, and you shall prune your vineyard six years, and gather in the fruit of it. [4] But in **the seventh year shall be a sabbath of rest to the land**, a sabbath for Jehovah. You shall neither sow your field, nor prune your vineyard. (*MKJV*)

God was making a specific promise to Israelites entering the Promised Land. In essence, He promised that if the Israelites would give the land a rest every seventh year, He would ensure a sufficient harvest in the sixth year to carry them through.

How long has it been since *you* voluntarily took a year off work to rest and worship the Lord? Except for some in the academic community, almost nobody takes a sabbatical year off work anymore. We should. It would do us good. I'm praying for the Lord's guidance in how my wife and I can do this.

In the very next chapter, Leviticus 26, God warned the Israelites what would happen if they did not obey God's Law, including His Sabbath rests:

> [27] And if ye will not for all this hearken unto me, but walk contrary unto me; [28] Then I will walk contrary unto you also in fury; and I, even I, will chastise you seven times for your sins . . . [33] And I will scatter you among the heathen, and will draw out a sword after you: and your land shall be desolate, and your cities waste. [34] **Then shall the land enjoy her sabbaths,** as long as it lieth desolate, and ye *be* in your enemies' land; *even* then shall the land rest, and enjoy her sabbaths. [35] As long as it lieth desolate it shall rest; because it did not rest in your sabbaths, when ye dwelt upon it.

Unfortunately, the Israelites did not have enough faith to claim this promise. Therefore God allowed them to be carried captive so the land could enjoy sabbaths in their absence, as we see in 2 Chronicles chapter 36:

> [11] Zedekiah *was* twenty-one years old when he began to reign, and he reigned eleven years in Jerusalem. [12] And he did the evil in the sight of Jehovah his God. He was not humbled before Jeremiah the prophet, from the mouth of Jehovah. [13] And he also rebelled against King Nebuchadnezzar, who had made him swear by God. But he stiffened his neck and hardened his heart from turning to Jehovah, the God of Israel. [14] Also all the chief of the priests, and the people, transgressed very much after all the abominations of the nations. And they polluted the house of Jehovah which He had made holy in Jerusalem. [15] And Jehovah, the God of their fathers sent to them by His messengers, rising up early and sending, for He had pity on His people and on His dwelling-place. [16] But they mocked the messengers of God and despised His words, and ill-treated His prophets until the wrath of Jehovah arose against His people, until there was no healing. [17] And He

caused the king of the Chaldeans to go up against them. And he killed their choice ones by the sword in the house of their holy place, and had no pity on the young man and the virgin, the old man and the very aged; He gave all into his hand. [18] And all the vessels of the house of God, great and small, and the treasures of the house of Jehovah, and the treasures of the king, and of his rulers, he brought all these to Babylon. [19] And they burned the house of God, and broke down the wall of Jerusalem, and burned all the palaces of it with fire, and destroyed all its beautiful vessels. [20] And the ones who had escaped from the sword he carried away to Babylon, where they were servants to him and his sons until the reign of the kingdom of Persia, [21] to fulfill the Word of Jehovah in the mouth of Jeremiah, until the land had enjoyed its sabbaths. All the days of the desolation it kept the sabbath, to the full measure of seventy years. (MKJV)

What amazes me is that God continued to love the people of Israel, despite their disobedience. Even after they were carried away to exile, He continued to send His word to them through His prophets. Of particular interest to us in the 21st century is the message recorded in Jeremiah 29:

[4] So says the Lord of Hosts, the God of Israel, to all the exiles whom I caused to be exiled from Jerusalem to Babylon: [5] Build houses and live *in them*; and plant gardens and eat their fruit. [6] Take wives and father sons and daughters. And take wives for your sons, and give your daughters to husbands, so that they may bear sons and daughters, that you may be multiplied there and not become few. [7] And seek the peace of the city where I have caused you to be exiled, and pray to Jehovah for it. For in its peace you shall have peace. [8] For so says Jehovah of Hosts, the God of Israel: Do not let your prophets and your fortune-tellers in your midst deceive you, nor listen to your dreams which you dream. [9] For they prophesy falsely to you in My name; I have not sent them, says Jehovah. [10] For so says Jehovah, When according to My Word seventy years have been fulfilled for Babylon, I will visit you and confirm My good Word to you, to bring you back to this place. [11] For I know the purposes which I am purposing for you, says Jehovah; purposes of peace and not of evil, to give you a future and a hope. [12] Then you shall call on Me, and you shall go and pray to Me, and I will listen to you. [13] And you shall seek Me and find *Me*, when you search for Me with all your heart. *(MKJV)*

We must pay special heed to this message, because our nation has become as evil as pre-exile Judah. Because of our sins, God has allowed the present-day Babylonians (fanatical Muslim terrorists) to attack the United States and Israel, to cause us to turn back to Him.

Without a widespread repentance and revival, the United States is at risk of being destroyed in the holocaust described in Ezekiel Chapters 38 and 39. If you are not familiar with this upcoming battle, please read about it online at www.BibleWriter.com/revelation16.htm.

Despite our sins, God calls us to turn to Him, as we see in verses 12 and 13: "Then you shall call on Me, and you shall go and pray to Me, and I will listen to you. And you shall seek Me and find Me, when you search for Me with all your heart." (*MKJV*)

Closing Prayer: Lord, my worship often comes short of Your standards, and my love for you has not been consistent. I repent of my lukewarm personal devotions and my selfish prayers. Please open my eyes to see Your plan, and open my ears to hear Your Holy Spirit's gentle leading, I pray in Jesus' name. Amen.

Chapter 18

Bema Rewards

Why are we doing this?

> Then answered Peter and said unto Him, "Behold, we have forsaken all, and followed Thee; what shall we have therefore?" *Matthew 19:27*

Opening Prayer: Lord, eternity sounds a long ways off. With Your help, I can hold on until then. But tell me again why I'm doing this?

Most of us enjoy reading about Simon Peter. He asks the same questions and makes some of the same mistakes that we do. This man followed Jesus with all his heart, as a full-time disciple. But even Peter found it difficult to see past the cares of this life and grasp future reality.

Let's review the full story in Matthew 19. Jesus had just spoken with the rich young ruler, who had left in sorrow because he was unable to part with his millions of shekels:

> [23] Then said Jesus unto His disciples, "Verily I say unto you, that a rich man shall hardly enter into the kingdom of Heaven. [24] And again I say unto you, it is easier for a camel to go through the eye of a needle than for a rich man to enter into the kingdom of God." [25] When His disciples heard *it*, they were exceedingly amazed, saying, "Who then can

be saved?"[26] But Jesus beheld *them*, and said unto them, "With men this is impossible; but with God all things are possible." [27] Then answered Peter and said unto Him, "Behold, we have forsaken all, and followed Thee; what shall we have therefore?"

Remember the context. The nation of Israel was anticipating a political messiah who would lead the nation into a time of military and spiritual greatness. Jesus' disciples expected to participate as high executives in Jesus' kingdom.

The disciples expected rewards of wealth and power. Peter and John had walked away from a successful fishing business. Matthew had abandoned a profitable tax franchise. But if money was an obstacle to entering the promised Kingdom, then what rewards could His disciples expect when the Kingdom arrived? The Lord's answer was reassuring:

[28] And Jesus said unto them, "Verily I say unto you, that ye which have followed me, in the regeneration when the Son of man shall sit in the throne of his glory, ye also shall sit upon twelve thrones, judging the twelve tribes of Israel. [29] "And every one that hath forsaken houses, or brethren, or sisters, or father, or mother, or wife, or children, or lands, for my name's sake, shall receive an hundredfold, and shall inherit everlasting life. [30] "But many that are first shall be last; and the last shall be first."

The point is clear. God will give us a hundredfold blessing if we trust Him, and He will allow us to enter into His eternal Kingdom.

Just being in Heaven will be wonderful, and the Lord will give us positions of authority based on our faithfulness. But none of our credit cards or cash will buy anything in Heaven. In fact, our dogged pursuit of money can keep us *out* of Heaven unless we surrender our hearts and checkbooks—now—to the Lordship of Jesus Christ.

The gospel of Mark has a parallel passage in chapter 10, and it sheds additional light:

[29] And Jesus answered and said, "Truly I say to you, there is no man that has left house or brothers or sisters or father or mother or wife or children or lands for my sake and the gospel's sake, [30] "but he shall receive a hundredfold now in this time, houses and brothers and sisters and mothers and children and lands with persecutions, and in the world to come, eternal life. [31] "But many that are first shall be last; and the last shall be first." (MKJV)

Notice that verse 30 of Mark's account adds two tiny details:

- Hundredfold rewards will be received "now in this time." While we probably not receive 100 new houses or brothers before we die, we will certainly receive blessings from God. He will always bring joy to a submitted heart, and He might also bring material blessings.

- The hundredfold rewards will arrive "with persecutions." Our enemy and his servants will attack you mercilessly for preferring Jesus to this world. They will think *you* have it backwards, and will hate you for it. Take heart. Jesus will love you for it.

Jesus will bless you in this life, but He wants you to concentrate on eternal rewards. He wants to give you eternal gifts at His Bema seat.

What is a Bema?

In the Greco-Roman culture, there was a judgment seat—the Greek word was *bema*—where government officials decided matters of law. We see an example in Scripture in Matthew 27:

> [15] Now at *that* feast the governor was accustomed to release to the people a prisoner, whomever they desired. [16] And they then had a notorious prisoner called Barabbas. [17] Therefore when they were gathered together, Pilate said to them, "Whom do you desire that I release to you? Barabbas, or Jesus *who is* called Christ?" [18] For he knew they had delivered Him because of envy. [19] But as he was sitting down on the **judgment seat** (*bema*), his wife sent to him, saying, "Have nothing to do with that just man, for today because of Him I have suffered many things in a dream." (MKJV)

The word is sometimes translated *throne* as we see in Acts chapter 12:

> [20] And Herod was in bitter hostility with the men of Tyre and Sidon. But they came to him with one accord and, having made Blastus (who had charge of the king's bedroom) their friend, desired peace, because their country was fed by the king's *country*. [21] And on a certain day, Herod sat on his **throne** (*bema*), dressed in royal clothing, and made a speech to them. [22] And the people gave a shout, *saying, "It* is the voice of a god and not of a man!" [23] And immediately the angel of *the* Lord

struck him, because he did not give God the glory. And he was eaten by worms and gave up the spirit. *(MKJV)*

A third example can be found in Acts chapter 25:

⁴ Then indeed Festus answered that Paul should be kept at Caesarea; he himself would depart shortly. ⁵ Then he said, those having power among you may go down with *me*. If there is a thing amiss in this man, let them accuse him. ⁶ And staying among them more than ten days, going down to Caesarea, on the next day sitting on the **judgment seat** *(bema)*, he commanded Paul to be brought. *(MKJV)*

In these three examples, *bema* describes a seat of judicial or legal authority. The word *bema* also described the seat of honor at sporting events. High government officials would preside over the contests from the *bema* and give rewards to the winners.

Paul used *bema* to describe the place where Jesus will sit to give rewards to believers, in his second letter to the Corinthians, chapter 5:

⁶ Therefore *we are* always confident, knowing that, whilst we are at home in the body, we are absent from the Lord: ⁷ (For we walk by faith, not by sight:) ⁸ We are confident, *I say*, and willing rather to be absent from the body, and to be present with the Lord. ⁹ Wherefore we labour, that, whether present or absent, we may be accepted of him. ¹⁰ For we must all appear before the **judgment seat** *(bema)* of Christ; that every one may receive the things *done* in *his* body, according to that he hath done, whether *it be* good or bad.

To understand this passage, you must understand the context. Paul is talking to believers, using the personal pronoun "we" eight times in these 5 verses. More importantly, Paul is talking about rewards given to believers. He is *not* talking about the issue of salvation.

We believers have already resolved the issue of salvation, and we have received that reward already. We gained assurance of salvation when we began trusting in the completed work of Jesus, the Messiah. We are either saved or not saved, as explained in the early chapters of this book. Instead, Paul is talking about rewards we receive in "the life to come" that Jesus mentioned.

Notice also the concept presented in verses 6 through 8. While we are present (alive) in this physical body, we are absent from the Lord's presence in Heaven. Soon we will be absent from this body and present with the Lord in Heaven.

The flavor of this passage is that we go to Heaven and receive rewards immediately after our physical death. This is consistent with the imagery of an Olympic sporting event, where the winner gets his medal in a ceremony soon after his or her victory.

Paul reinforces this concept of specific rewards in his second letter to Timothy, chapter 4:

> [6] For I am now ready to be offered, and the time of my departure is at hand. [7] I have fought a good fight, I have finished my course, I have kept the faith. [8] Henceforth there is laid up for me a crown of righteousness, which the Lord, the righteous Judge, shall give me at that day, and not to me only, but unto all them also that love His appearing.

Paul is ready for his "departure"—the Greek word is *analusis*, used of a ship leaving port to begin a journey. Paul is ready to be absent from the body and present with the Lord, because he is confident that he will receive rewards from the Lord.

Notice that Paul talks of receiving a crown—the word is *stephanos* in the Greek. It was a special wreath given as a prize in the public games or worn by royalty generally. It was a more conspicuous and elaborate wreath than the simple *diadema* given to lesser dignitaries.

When is the bema?

The Scriptures aren't crystal clear on this point, so there's room for honest disagreement concerning the timing. One group argues that the *bema* is an individual event, taking place immediately after each person's death. Others say it will happen at the time of the first Rapture event, or at the Marriage Supper of the Lamb. Others believe it will happen after Jesus physically returns to earth, because of the wording of verse 8. So who is right?

My vote is "all the above." The Scriptures do not require any of the above positions to be the "all-or-nothing" truth. Instead, it seems logical that we would get rewards and recognition from the Lord at each of the above events. The important issue isn't when we get rewarded but if we get rewards and what the rewards will be.

Paul also speaks of rewards in the third chapter of his first letter to the Corinthians:

> [8] Now he that planteth and he that watereth are one: and every man shall receive his own reward according to his own labour. [9] For we are labourers together with God: ye are God's husbandry, *ye are* God's build-

ing. [10] According to the grace of God which is given unto me, as a wise masterbuilder, I have laid the foundation, and another buildeth thereon. But let every man take heed how he buildeth thereupon. [11] For other foundation can no man lay than that is laid, which is Jesus Christ. [12] Now if any man build upon this foundation gold, silver, precious stones, wood, hay, stubble; [13] Every man's work shall be made manifest: for the day shall declare it, because it shall be revealed by fire; and the fire shall try every man's work of what sort it is. [14] If any man's work abide which he hath built thereupon, he shall receive a reward. [15] If any man's work shall be burned, he shall suffer loss: but he himself shall be saved; yet so as by fire.

Notice verse 12: we have a choice of building materials to work with. Then notice verse 15: our work will be tested by fire.

The meaning is clear. If we are following Jesus with all our heart, abiding in Him daily, we are building with precious materials that will survive fire—gold, silver and precious stones.

If we are saved but just getting by with the bare minimum, we are building with wood, hay and straw—materials that will vanish into smoke at the *bema* judgment. We ourselves will be saved and will enter into eternity with Jesus. But we will have an eternity to regret the missed opportunities to gain eternal treasure.

Jesus is not impressed by appearances or by worldly success. Jesus looks at our hearts, and sees what fruit we have brought forth, as we have submitted to the leading of the Holy Spirit. We see these words in Matthew 7:

[17] Even so every good tree bringeth forth good fruit; but a corrupt tree bringeth forth evil fruit. [18] A good tree cannot bring forth evil fruit, neither can a corrupt tree bring forth good fruit. [19] Every tree that bringeth not forth good fruit is hewn down, and cast into the fire. [20] Wherefore by their fruits ye shall know them.

For a reality check, you should re-read the earlier chapter, "Fruit of the Holy Spirit." And remember that Jesus wants you to bear *much* fruit for His glory.

Many big-name TV ministers will be surprised to watch their works go "poof!" at the *bema* seat. Many have built fancy studios and collected millions of dollars by preaching messages that emphasize material prosperity. Some claim to exercise "healing power" and "words of prophecy" in the name of Jesus. Unfortunately, some of these hirelings will have a rude shock coming, as we see in the next verses of Matthew 7:

> [21] "Not every one that saith unto me, 'Lord, Lord' shall enter into the kingdom of Heaven; but he that doeth the will of my Father which is in Heaven. [22] "Many will say to me in that day, 'Lord, Lord, have we not prophesied in thy name? and in thy name have cast out devils? and in thy name done many wonderful works?' [23] "And then will I profess unto them, 'I never knew you: depart from me, ye that work iniquity.'"

The prophet Ezekiel had a similar problem with religious phonies in his day. There were Levites (the priestly class) who diligently performed the external rituals of the priesthood, but whose hearts were not right before God. These Levites were mercenaries, doing their good deeds to be seen by men, and to receive financial rewards.

In Ezekiel 44, we read God's explanation of how these Levites would be rewarded during the 1,000-year reign of Christ:

> [10] And the Levites that are gone away far from me, when Israel went astray, which went astray away from me after their idols; they shall even bear their iniquity. [11] Yet they shall be ministers in My sanctuary, having charge at the gates of the house, and ministering to the house: they shall slay the burnt offering and the sacrifice for the people, and they shall stand before them to minister unto them. [12] Because they ministered unto them before their idols, and caused the house of Israel to fall into iniquity; therefore have I lifted up mine hand against them, saith the Lord GOD, and they shall bear their iniquity.
>
> [13] And they shall not come near unto Me, to do the office of a priest unto Me, nor to come near to any of My holy things, in the most holy place: but they shall bear their shame, and their abominations which they have committed. [14] But I will make them keepers of the charge of the house, for all the service thereof, and for all that shall be done therein.

Since salvation is by faith and not by works, God will honor the "saved" status of many of today's hireling TV ministers. However, they will do the "grunt" work of the temple—sacrificing animals, sweeping floors, picking up trash and ministering to the needs of the people. They are devoted to the external trappings of ministry today, and will be trapped in superficial tasks after Christ returns.

Notice the chilling words of verse 13: "They shall not come near unto Me, to do the office of a priest unto Me, nor to come near to any of My holy things, in the most holy place." These men and women are not seeking God in His secret place today. They are not abiding in Christ today. They will not be allowed in His presence in the life to come.

By contrast, note what the Lord says about those of us who work faithfully, in obscurity, seeking God early in the morning while the charlatans sleep:

> [15] But the priests the Levites, the sons of Zadok, that kept the charge of My sanctuary when the children of Israel went astray from Me, they shall come near to Me to minister unto Me, and they shall stand before Me to offer unto Me the fat and the blood, saith the Lord GOD: [16] They shall enter into My sanctuary, and they shall come near to My table, to minister unto Me, and they shall keep My charge.

Note how many times the Lord says "Me" and "My" in these verses. He notices who is serving Him faithfully. He intends to keep His faithful servants near Him for all eternity.

This should encourage pastors (and their wives) who have faithfully served God in tiny churches, proclaiming the gospel of Jesus and daily seeking His presence and guidance. This should also encourage Sunday School workers and home group leaders and others who have never received recognition for their works.

If we are faithful to abide in Christ today, when nobody seems to notice or care, Jesus will honor us publicly in the near future. Better yet, He will allow us to abide in His presence in the life to come.

Soon we will experience the reality of Revelation chapter 21:

> [3] And I heard a great voice out of Heaven saying, "Behold, the tabernacle of God is with men, and He will dwell with them, and they shall be His people, and God Himself shall be with them, and be their God. [4] And God shall wipe away all tears from their eyes; and there shall be no more death, neither sorrow, nor crying, neither shall there be any more pain: for the former things are passed away.

Difficult as they seem, our present problems are what God calls "the former things." Distant as they seem, the blessings of Revelation 21 should be our reality.

Abide faithfully in Him today, and we shall soon have durable, everlasting joy in His presence—at the *bema* and forever.

Closing Prayer: Lord, I repent of the opportunities that I've missed, and the ways I have come short in the past. Help me, by Your Spirit, to abide in Your love and Your grace that I may minister to You in eternity. I pray this in Jesus'mighty name. Amen.

Chapter 19

Joy Without End, Amen

"Are we there yet, Daddy?"

"Follow Me." *Matthew 4:19*

Opening Prayer: Lord, what must I do now?

By now, you have been shown the secret of durable joy. But do you truly understand it? Have you grasped the fact that faith is your key to peace and joy that will never end?

God is calling you to either trust your human logic or commit to following His formula for your joy:

- Your logical mind tells you that Jesus spoke in odd parables. Faith tells you that Jesus hid the truth in plain sight.
- Your logical mind realizes that you can never be good enough to gain heaven in your own strength. Faith tells you that you must be born again (receive a supernatural heart transplant) in order to qualify for heaven and become a vessel of God's joy.

- Your human emotions tell you that it's fun to rebel against the rules, especially God's. Faith tells you that the greatest joy is in complete obedience and submission.

- Your human logic and emotions drive you to compete with your friends and co-workers. Faith tells you that the greatest joy comes in serving others, and that pride disqualifies you from effective ministry.

- Your human logic and emotions cause you to like and dislike different individuals. Faith tells you that joy comes when you learn to love people because Jesus loves them and died on their behalf.

Let me encourage you to put your faith in the character and faithfulness of the God of Abraham, Isaac and Jacob. Follow Jesus with all your heart, and your joy will be eternal.

Closing Prayer: Lord, I commit my heart to Your service. Make me an instrument of Your peace and joy. Amen.

To order additional copies of

DURABLE JOY
Mysteriously Hidden in Plain Sight

Have your credit card ready and call:

1-877-421-READ (7323)

or please visit our web site at
www.pleasantword.com

Also available at: www.amazon.com

Printed in the United States
786500005B